creative
Crocheted Dolls

50 Whimsical Designs

Noreen Crone-Findlay

Published by

 **krause publications**
An F+W Publications Company

700 East State Street • Iola, WI 54990-0001
715-445-2214 • 888-457-2873
www.krause.com

To place an order or obtain a free catalog, please call 800-258-0929.

Library of Congress Catalog Number: 2004100942
ISBN: 0-87349-741-4

Designed by Marilyn McGrane and Donna Mummery
Edited by Christine Townsend

Dedicated

To the memory of my cousin, Debra Grimes, and of course to my darling beloveds: Jim, Chloe, and Angus, and my Momsie and Popsie, and to my sweet Mum-in-law, Grace, and also my sibs, David, Lesley-Ann, and Jonathan. AND! To all those who love the creative potential of crochet.

Grateful Thanks

To dear friends: Ardis Johnson, Terri Christiansen—Bibby, Nathalie Schiebel, Aleksa Harkness, Silvie Nicolas, Judy and Jim Wood, Patricia Wallace, Rainbow Lynne MacKay, Jana Willow, Sandy Fitzgerald, and Tish Murphy.

To the Fairy Godmothers of this book: Julie Stephani, Gwen Blakely-Kinsler, and Nancy Brown.

I also am very grateful to the Spinrite/Bernat company for their gracious and generous support over the years. It is most appreciated. And I would especially like to thank Sara Arblaster in particular.
Another really gracious sponsor is Maureen Dow of Cedar Hollow Looms. They make the most beautiful tools you can imagine.

To the terrific team at Krause who helped to co-create this book: Christine Townsend and Niki Gould, editors extraordinaire; Robert Best, the appropriately named photographer; Marilyn McGrane and Donna Mummery, the book designers. I also want to thank all the other wonderful people at Krause Publications who worked so hard to make this book happen.

Acknowledgments

I appreciate the kindness and generous support of the following companies, who supplied me with the things that allowed me to create the projects in the book:

Bernat/Spinright: Yarn
Cedar Hollow Looms: Hand-dyed mohair roving and locks
CGOA Presents: Yarn, buttons, beads
Fancifuls Inc.: Brass charms and embellishments
Fleece Artist: Hand dyed rovings, yarn
Heritan: Fine hemp cord, pin backs, copper foil and embossing tool
Lee Valley: Nylon cord, wood-burning tool, wood veneer, jute, craft knives, copper ornaments, raffia
Skacel: Crochet hooks
Staples/Business Depot: Nifty paperclips, crayons, and pencil crayons
Turn of the Century: Hand-tuned wooden crochet hooks
Walnut Hollow: Versatool

An Apology

We've tried to make this book as free of errors as possible. But sometimes the gremlins dance, and glitches spring up. If there are mistakes, I apologize for them.

Table of Contents

Introduction

Fairy Godmothers

Not too long ago, I had a dream in which a Fairy Godmother appeared. With a great flourish of fairy dust, she tossed a magic wand to me. I leapt up to catch it and was delighted to find that the magic wand was actually a crochet hook with a star on the end! The Fairy Godmother chortled at me, "Well now, what are you going to make of this?" and vanished. What *am* I going to make of this? Dolls, of course!

About a year later, a different kind of Fairy Godmother asked me another really good question. This time, I was awake, and the Fairy Godmother was Gwen Blakely-Kinsler. Gwen, who founded the Crochet Guild of America (bless her), spoke admiringly of several wonderful new cloth dollmaking books. She asked where the new *crochet* doll book was. She had planted the seed! We talked through e-mails and on the phone, and soon, the seed burst into bloom! I got more and more excited about the idea of writing a book about creative crocheted dolls, and the little thought grew and grew.

Gwen also brought another "Fairy Godmother" into the picture: Nancy Brown. Nancy is a bubbly, vivacious dynamo and is at the heart of the "CGOA Presents" yarn section of the Crochet Guild of America. Nancy and I had wonderful conversations about the direction of the book. She helped enormously in its gestation. She also supplied many of the gorgeous yarns that I have used in the book.

And, lucky ducky that I am, I have yet *another* Fairy Godmother: Julie Stephani, the acquisitions editor at Krause. Amazingly enough, Julie had been one of the founding members of the Crochet Guild of America. Bless her darling heart, she also was excited about a book of creative crocheted dolls. Julie truly put the wheels and the wings on the book.

We all need to have Fairy Godmothers who will inspire, delight, support, and ask us important questions! I hope that all your sweetest dreams come true and that you will always know that *your* Fairy Godmothers are there for you!

A note about the structure of the book: Because this is a book about the creative process, I began with a simple little doll and then followed the promptings and questions that came up as one idea naturally led to another. I've had a wonderful time playing with those ideas, and then designing and crocheting the dolls that sprang from those musings. I hope that this book and the dolls in it will inspire you to create your own unique, one-of-a-kind, *Creative Crocheted Dolls*.

A Brief Discussion of the Basics

The Crochet Guild of America has a comprehensive crocheting tutorial on its Web site: www.crochet.org.

The Stitches

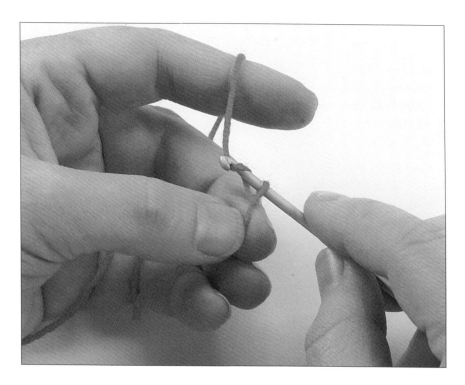

Chain Stitch

Abbreviation: **ch**

Make a loop. Place the loop on the hook.
Catch the yarn and pull it through the loop on the hook.

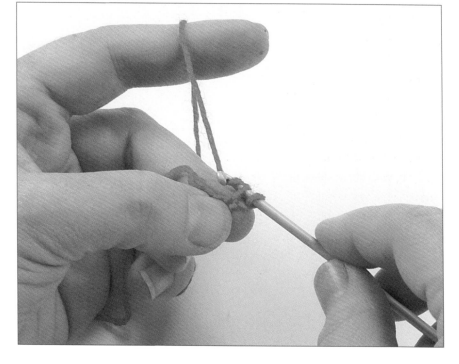

Slip Stitch

Abbreviation: **sl st**

Insert the hook into a previous stitch, and take yarn over the hook.
Pull the yarn through both the stitch and the loop on the hook.
This is how you join the end of a row to the starting stitch of the row.

Single Crochet

Abbreviation: **sc**

1. Insert the hook from front to back into a chain or stitch in the previous row of stitches; take yarn over hook. Pull through the chain or stitch (two loops on hook).

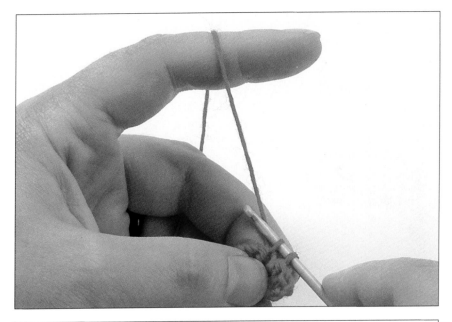

2. Yarn over hook and pull through both loops on hook.

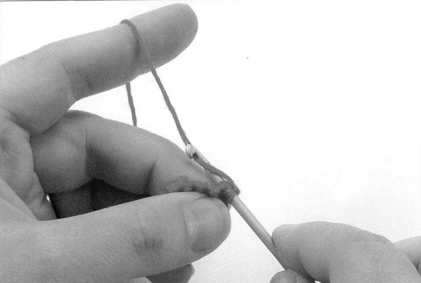

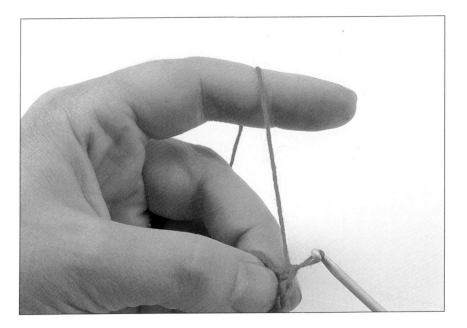

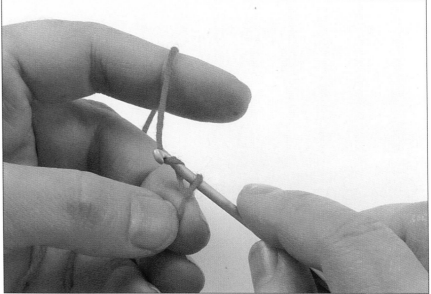

Half-double Crochet

Abbreviation: **hdc**

1. Yarn over hook, and insert hook
into stitch in previous row.
Pull up through the stitch, forming
three loops on hook.

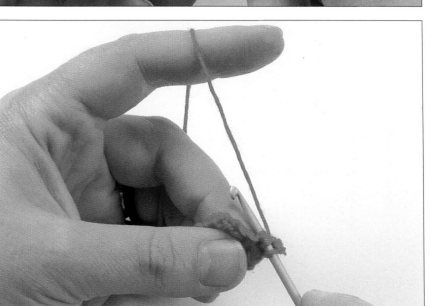

2. Yarn over and pull through all three
loops.

Double Crochet

Abbreviation: **dc**

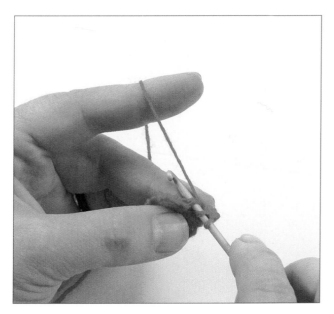

1. Yarn over, insert hook into stitch in previous row.

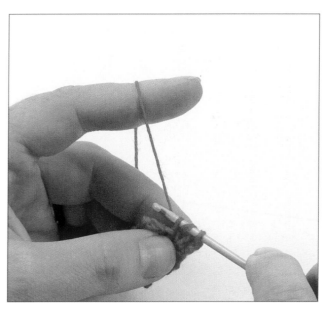

2. Yarn over again and pull yarn through chain or stitch (three loops on hook).

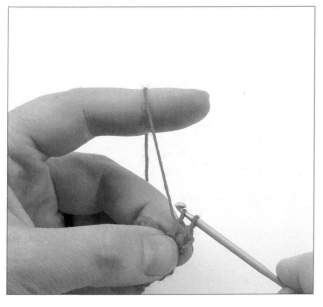

3. Yarn over and pull through two loops.

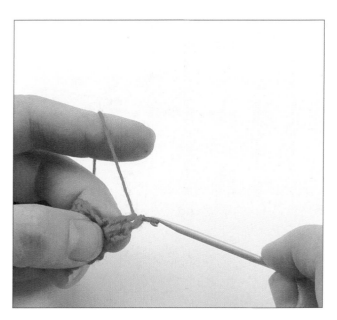

4. Yarn over and pull through two loops again.

Triple or Treble Crochet

Abbreviation: **tr**

1. Yarn over twice, insert hook into stitch of previous row.

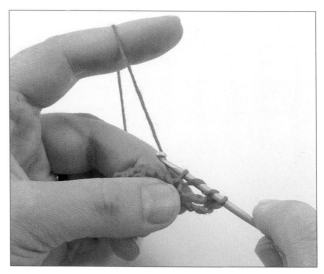

2. Yarn over again and pull yarn through stitch (four loops on hook).

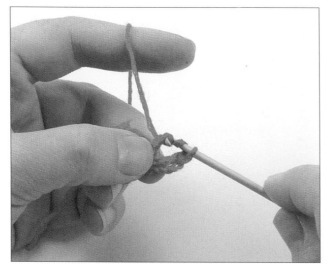

3. Yarn over and pull through two loops.

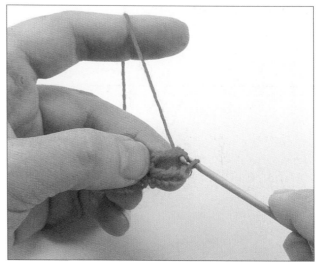

4. Yarn over and pull through two loops again.

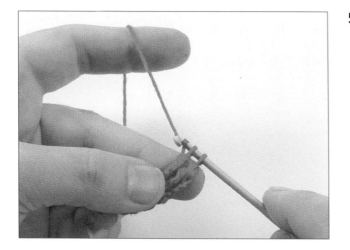

5. Yarn over and pull through the last two loops for a third time.

Other Standard Crochet Abbreviations

inc = increase
dec = decrease
yo = yarn over

Some Useful Embroidery Stitches

Couching

The outline is made by one thread, and another is used to stitch it in place. This is a really good way to draw faces. Traditionally, you would stitch over and over the outline thread. But, when you are drawing faces with couching, it's okay to break a few rules, and space the "capturing" stitches just where you need them to hold the shape.

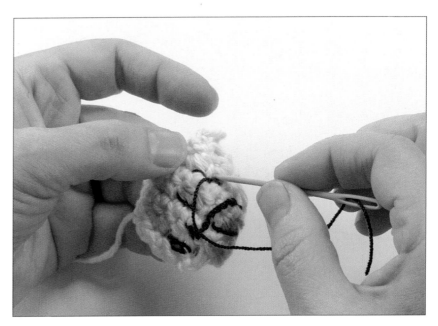

Daisy Stitch

1. Bring the yarn out at the base of the petal, and take the needle back in at the base, coming out at the tip of the petal. Bring the yarn around the needle, forming the petal. Pull the needle through.

2. Take a tiny stitch at the end of the petal to anchor it, then bring the needle back out at the base of the petal to begin the next petal.

Stitching Pieces Together

One of the best methods of stitching pieces together is to use the Baseball stitch. It is a "V"-shaped stitch that disappears into the fabric. Here's how:

1. With the edges of the pieces held together, anchor the end of the stitching yarn or thread by sewing over and over in one place on one of the pieces.

2. Take the needle into the space between the two pieces and bring it up from the inside to the outside of the piece. Pull up the length of yarn.

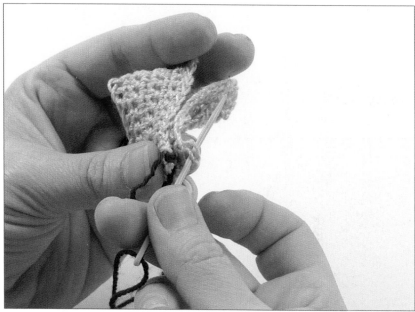

3. Take the needle back down into the space between the two pieces and bring it up from the inside of the other piece to the outside.

4. Repeat steps 2 and 3 until seam is completely sewn, and anchor last stitches, taking them inside to hide the ends.

chapter one

The Essentials of Creativity

Creativity requires tools. One of the most essential tools is a notebook. Small notebooks that can be easily carried are perfect. You can write down dreams, thoughts, quick sketches, and especially, questions as they pop up—this is important, as so much of creativity is a response to the question, "What if?" If you stick a little flag on the edge of the page with a key word printed on it, you can quickly get to the idea and start working with it.

Other tools essential for the explorations of creativity in this book are: pencils, erasers, permanent pens, erasable markers, paper clips, glue, scissors, pencil crayons, wax crayons, wood-burning tools, paper punches, and needle-nose pliers. The most essential element, however, is the Creative Attitude.

The Creative Attitude is the mindset that chooses to be diligent in the pursuit of creativity. The Creative Attitude is a commitment to being resilient, and a willingness to look at the world and find new ways of seeing and being.

The Essentials of Crochet: Hooks!

The crochet hook is an amazing and wonderful tool. It's elegant, and so simple—just a stick with a hook on the end, right? Yes, but consider the things you can do with this little, hooked stick! You can make very useful, everyday objects with the crochet hook, but there is so much more to it.

It is painterly, allowing us to create swirls and washes of glorious color. It is also a sculpting tool that enables us to build three-dimensional objects that touch our hearts, while expressing our dreams and the depths and heights of our souls. The hook can also connect us to our heritage, while we move our hands in the rhythms of our ancestors in creating the lacy webs of history. And, besides, it's just plain fun to crochet.

When you are choosing a hook for dollmaking, there are a few things to take into consideration. Your choice of hook depends on the doll you are making and the effect you wish to create. If you want a dense, sturdy fabric, then you will choose a hook that is one or even two sizes smaller than the one recommended on the yarn label. If you want a soft, lacy, or drapey fabric, choose a hook that is larger than the size recommended on the label of the yarn.

It doesn't matter if you prefer a metal hook, a wooden, or even a plastic one; let your own heart and hands make the choice. You can even make your own hooks—I did!

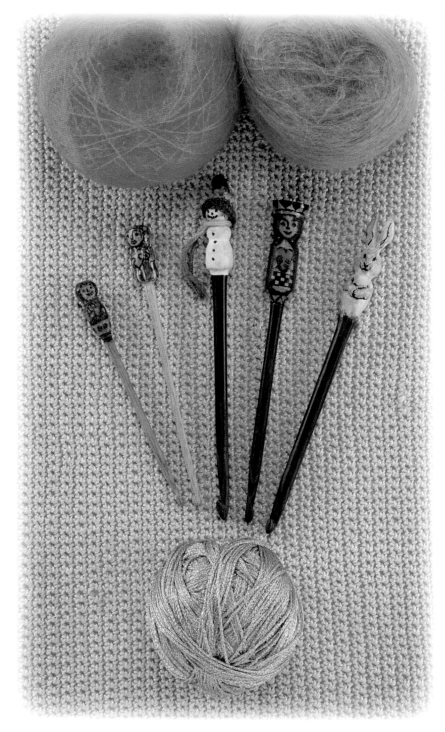

My son Angus turned the basic shape of these hooks on the lathe, and I carved the dolls on the ends, shaped the hooks, and painted them. I wasn't going to include them here, but my brother David really likes them. David convinced me to include them in the book. He said that it would inspire people to give it a try themselves. Hope he's right!

Paper Clip Glasses

Many hooks have *two* useful ends! What could you make with the other end of the crochet hook? You can make wonderful embellishments for your dolls. Here's one idea.

Instructions

1. Straighten a paper clip, or cut a length of wire about 3½" long.

2. About a ½" away from the center of the wire, wrap the wire around a 2mm or 2.5mm crochet hook to form the first lens. Note that the wire goes around the hook with the arm of the glasses to the back and the part of the wire that will go over the nose to the front.

Materials

- Plastic-covered paper clips or 18-gauge wire
- Needle-nose pliers with a cutting notch
- Tape measure
- 2mm or 2.5mm metal crochet hook with a plain end

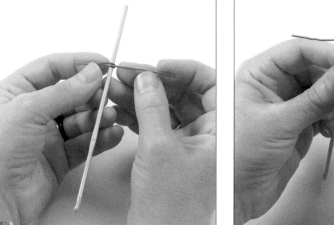

3. About ⅛" away from first lens, wrap wire around hook to form second lens. Wrap so that the "arm" wire goes behind the "nose" section of the glasses.

4. Bend curves at the end of the arms, using needle-nose pliers.

5. Fold the arms back. *Note: You can make larger glasses by using heavier-gauge wire and a larger crochet hook.*

Wire Coil Beads

Materials

- Plastic covered paper clips or 18-gauge wire
- Needle-nose pliers with a cutting notch
- Tape measure
- A metal crochet hook with a plain end

Instructions

Wrap 6" of wire around a 5mm (size H) crochet hook, pushing it together closely as you wrap. To make a longer bead, use a longer piece of wire.

Paper Beads

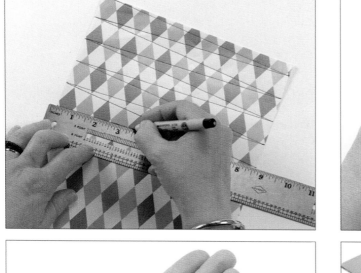

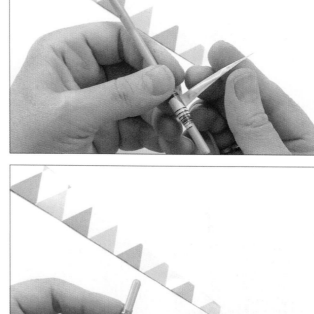

Instructions for making long tapered paper beads

1. Beginning at the long edge of one side of the paper, make a mark at each inch.
2. Along the other long edge, start ½" from the end of the paper and mark off each inch.
3. Connect the marks from one side of the paper to the other, forming long triangles.
4. Cut the triangles out with scissors.
5. Wrap the triangle around the hook, beginning with the wide end. After the first wrap, put a tiny dab of glue onto the paper.
6. Continue wrapping the paper around the hook. About 1" from the end, put a line of glue along the paper, and finish wrapping the bead.
7. Slip the bead off the hook. Trim the starting corners off the bead
8. Sometimes, the end will want to pop open. It's a good idea to hold it in place with a paper clip until it has dried.

Instructions for making short tubular paper beads

1. Cut ¼"-wide strips of paper. Wrap and glue them in the same way as the Long Tapered Beads (above).
2. If they pop open, clip them shut with a paper clip; remove the paper clip when the bead is completely dry.

Materials

- Damp cloth for cleaning fingers and crochet hook
- Ruler
- Scissors
- Decorative, colorful paper such as magazine pages
- 5mm (H) crochet hook
- Pencil
- Glue
- Paper clips

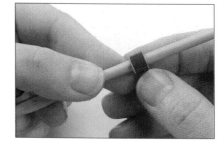

The dolls (from left to right) in this photo were made with: Doll #1: One strand of CGOA Presents Splendor #03 and a 2mm hook (finished size of doll: approximately 4"). Doll #2: One strand of CGOA Presents Splendor #03, plus one strand of CGOA Presents Kid Mohair #08 and a 2.5mm hook (finished size of doll: approximately 5-1/2"). Doll #3: One strand of CGOA Presents Splendor #03, plus one strand of CGOA Presents Kid Mohair #08, plus one strand CGOA Presents Sparkle #08 and a 3.5mm hook (finished size of doll: approximately 7½").

The Other Essential Tool: Yarn or Thread

How can you create your own yarn or thread? You can spin your own yarn, or combine threads and yarns (including sewing machine thread).

What could you use *instead* of yarn to make dolls? You can use jute, hemp, packing cord, string, bias tape, sewing machine thread, raffia … all kinds of things. How about using fabric strips? Reclaim and recycle old garments and fabric scraps by cutting them into strips and crocheting them. Cut the fabric into parallel strips; cut the strip almost up to the end of the piece of fabric. Move over ¼", and start a new strip by cutting down to the other end.

Swatches

A really valuable tool in the design process is the lowly and under-used swatch. Making swatches doesn't take a lot of time, and 10 stitches for 10 rows will give you a lot of design information. Crochet a heart from the graph on page 26; it works fine as a swatch, and then you can use it elsewhere in your dollmaking.

Swatching is a useful design tool, as it tells you which hook will work best with your yarn. If the fabric is too loopy and loose, then either switch to a smaller hook, or continue with the same hook and add another strand of thread or yarn to make the fabric denser. If the fabric of the swatch is too stiff, then switch to a larger hook.

Another Wonderful Tool: Graphs

One really good way of designing a doll is to sketch the shapes onto graph paper. But, it is really important to have graph paper that has the correct shape units, with the correct aspect ratio. Because crochet stitches tend to be taller than they are wide, the graph paper must have vertical rectangles. Square graph paper will give you a distorted finished product. When you are designing for crochet, and working directly onto graph paper, the grid should resemble the one in the lower right corner of the page.

Crocheting in Single Crochet from a Graph

Note: Row 1 and all odd-numbered rows are read from the right to the left. Row 2, and all even numbered rows are read from the left to the right. Each square or rectangle represents one single crochet.

1. Lay a ruler or strip of cardboard over Row 2, leaving Row 1 exposed. Move the cardboard strip up, one row at a time, so you can see the row you are working on, and the rows you've already done.
2. To begin, count the number of squares in Row 1. This is the lowest row on the graph. Chain that number, plus one (it gives you the height of the first sc in Row 2).
3. Beginning at the right hand side of Row 1, work one sc in the second ch from the hook and in each remaining ch. Ch 1 and turn.
4. When the graph moves out, add the same number of stitches to the row as squares. If it moves out one square, work 2 sc in the edge stitch.
5. When the graph moves in by one square at the beginning or end of a row, work a decrease over two stitches.
6. When it moves in by more than one square at the end of a row, work a dec over two stitches, then ch 1 and turn, leaving the remaining number of stitches unworked at the end of the row.

An Important Design Element: Faces

There are many ways of making unique and wonderful faces for dolls. Remember that leaving the face blank is also a totally acceptable option.

Start by designing the doll's face. With a blank piece of paper and a pencil, give yourself three or four minutes to scribble as many wild and crazy doodle faces as you can. Fill the page quickly with scratchy stick-men, blurry, silly,

terrible, goofy faces with eyes that are open and shut, mouths that are tiny and huge, ears that are tiny or missing, and noses that are long and short ... don't worry at all about how they look.

Keep playing with this exercise, and you'll find that you will develop a unique repertoire of faces that will lead to some amazing and pleasing dolls.

Borrow art and archeology books from the library, and look at the way the human face is depicted in different ways throughout history. Then, do the Face Scribble exercise again, and again! And, remember, the face doesn't have to be human and can be very abstract.

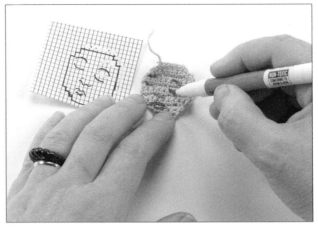

Embroidering Faces

You can embroider the face directly on the doll's head. I prefer to crochet a separate face, embroider it, and then appliqué it. Why? It's quicker to crochet the doll's head with one color, then crochet the face separately in another color and attach it. Also, you can crochet the face in a very fine gauge fabric and appliqué it to a larger-gauge fabric, which may have been too coarse to embroider comfortably on. And, you can alter the angle of the face, changing its expression. Here are graphs for some faces—a few ovals and a circle.

Copy the graphs and, using an erasable marker, draw some faces on the graph. Use the faces from the scribble exercise as a guide.

Following the graph, crochet the faces in single crochet. Sketch the face onto the crocheted face with an erasable marker. Embroider it with yarn, thread, or embroidery floss. (See Instructions for embroidery on page 12.)

Color the cheeks with blusher and the eyelids with eye shadow, or use pencil crayons. Stitch the face to the doll.

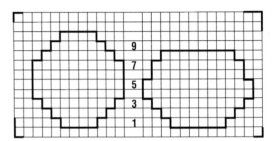

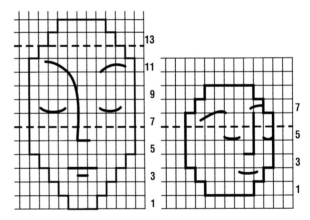

Carved Avocado Pit Faces

When I was writing *Soulmate Dolls: Dollmaking as a Healing Art*, I wanted to find a quick and easy way of carving faces. One day, when I was eating an avocado, I looked at the pit and had one of those "Aha!" moments! I was sure that this was the answer—and indeed it was! Avocado pits are easily carved. When they dry, they look very much like wood.

Instructions

1. Peel the brown skin from the avocado pit.
2. Find the "seam line," and pop the two halves apart.
3. With a ball-point pen, draw a rough outline of the face.
4. With a craft knife, carve the face.
5. Let dry thoroughly for a couple of weeks. It will shrink a lot.
6. The face can be sanded smooth. It can also be painted with acrylic paints.

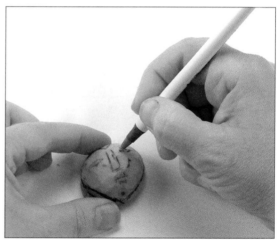

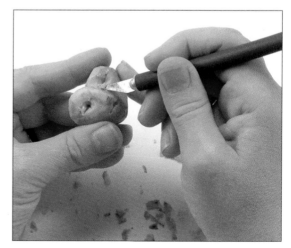

Brass Charms

Some brass charms make great heads for dolls. The ones in this book came from Fancifuls, Inc. To "antique" them, rub them with black acrylic paint, and buff the paint off before it's fully dry.

Hearts

Because creativity is about the connection among the heart, mind, and hands, the heart is one of the most important motifs in this book. These heart-shaped graphs will be used for many projects throughout the book.

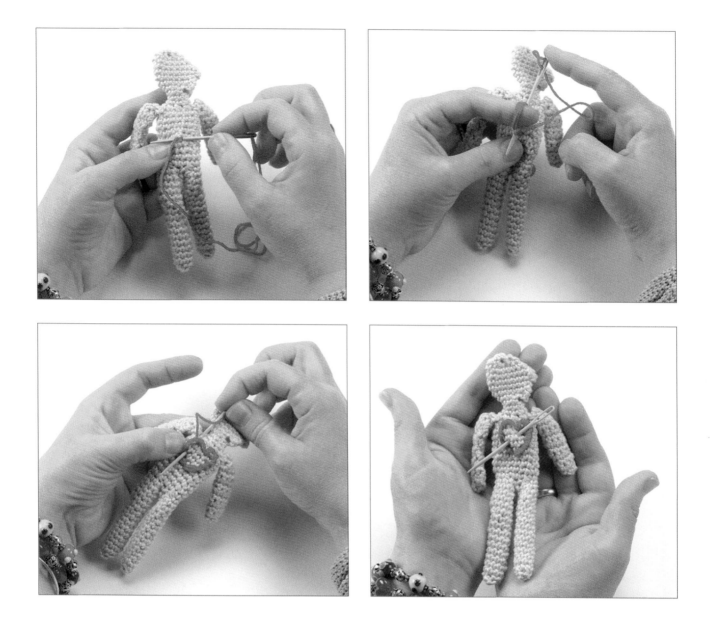

Instructions

1. Thread yarn or thread into a darning needle and take it inside the doll. Anchor it in place by stitching a couple of times in the same place on an inconspicuous spot.

2. Bring the needle out just above the doll's waist, (Point A) and place your finger on her chest. Stitch over your finger four times, or if your yarn is very thin, six times. The darning needle goes into the chest at Point B.

3. Divide the resulting loops in half, and fold them flat on the chest.

4. Stitch over the loops to shape and form the heart, securing them in place.

Hands and Feet

You can leave the hands and feet merely implied by not making them at all, or you can wrap yarn around the wrists and ankles, tie a knot, and then take the ends inside with a darning needle or crochet hook.

Crocheted Hands

Instructions

Begin: Ch 4, join, ch 1.

Row 1: 7 sc in ring, join, ch 1.

Row 2: 3 sc, 3 sc in next sc, 3 sc, join (9 sc).

Row 3: Thumb: Ch 4, 1 sl st in 2nd ch from hook, and in next 2 ch, 1 sc in each of 9 sc, join last sc to first sc, pushing thumb out of the way, ch 1.

Row 4: Skip first sc, 1 sc in remaining 8 sc, join last to first sc, ch 1.

Row 5: Fingers: Hold both layers of hand together and work fingers through both layers.

Pointer: 1 sc in first and 8th sc at the same time, ch 4, 1 sl st in 2nd ch from hook and in next 2 ch.

Middle: 1 sc in 2nd and 7th sc at the same time, ch 5, 1 sl st in 2nd ch from hook, and in next 3 ch.

Ring: 1 sc in 3rd and 6th sc at the same time, ch 4, 1 sl st in 2nd ch from hook and in next 2 ch.

Pinkie: 1 sc in 4th and 5th sc at the same time, ch 3, 1 sl st in 2nd ch from hook and in next ch and in side of sc below finger. Cut yarn, pull end through last loop on hook and weave end into hand.

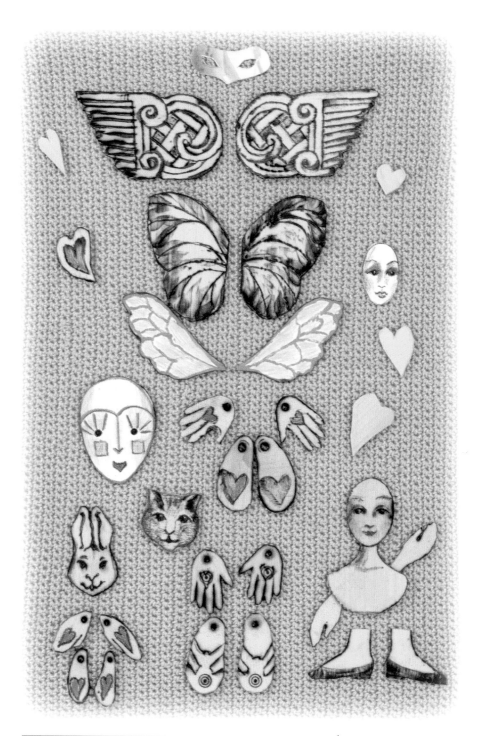

Making Hearts, Wings, Hands, Feet, Masks, and Faces in Wood and Paper

Patterns for elegant hands and feet, folkloric hands and feet, small hands and feet, fairy wings, butterfly wings, and Celtic wings are included on pages 31 and 32.

Instructions

1. Make a template: Copy the patterns onto paper, and glue them to lightweight cardboard. Cut them out. Cut out the heart on the hands and feet to make it easier to trace the hearts.
2. Trace around the template onto the paper or wood veneer that you are using to make the heart, hands, feet, wings, or face.
3. Or, use carbon paper to trace the pattern onto wood or paper.
4. To transfer to wood: Veneer is great because it can be cut with a craft knife or heavy scissors, so you don't need a saw. Glue veneer to one or both sides of thin non-corrugated cardboard, and clamp it with lots of paper clips or spring clamps to prevent curling.

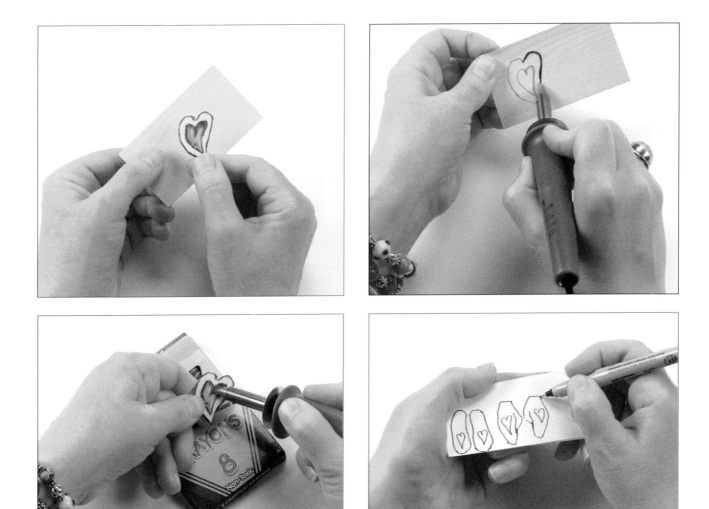

5. Let it dry completely. Glue veneer to just one side of the cardboard if it's a heart, or a face that will be glued to the doll. If you'll be able to see both sides (hands, feet, wings) then glue veneer to both sides of the cardboard. Burn design with a wood-burning tool.

6. Color the hearts with wax crayons, then lightly touch with the wood-burning tool to melt wax and set colors.

7. To transfer to paper: Watercolor paper or other heavy paper (such as old business cards) works best. Glue it to one or both sides of lightweight cardboard to strengthen it. Clamp with paper clips until it's dry. Cut out. Color with pencil or wax crayons.

Attaching Hands and Feet
Instructions

1. Pierce a hole in the top of each of the hands and feet. For the wooden ones, make the hole with the wood burner.

2. To join the hands and feet to the body, cut four pieces of 1" wide ribbon that are each 2" long (or you can use yarn or cord).

3. Thread them through the hole in the hand or foot and pull the ends up even.

4. Push the ends of the ribbon up inside the arm or leg, and push glue on both sides of the ribbon inside the wrist or ankle, to secure the hand or foot.

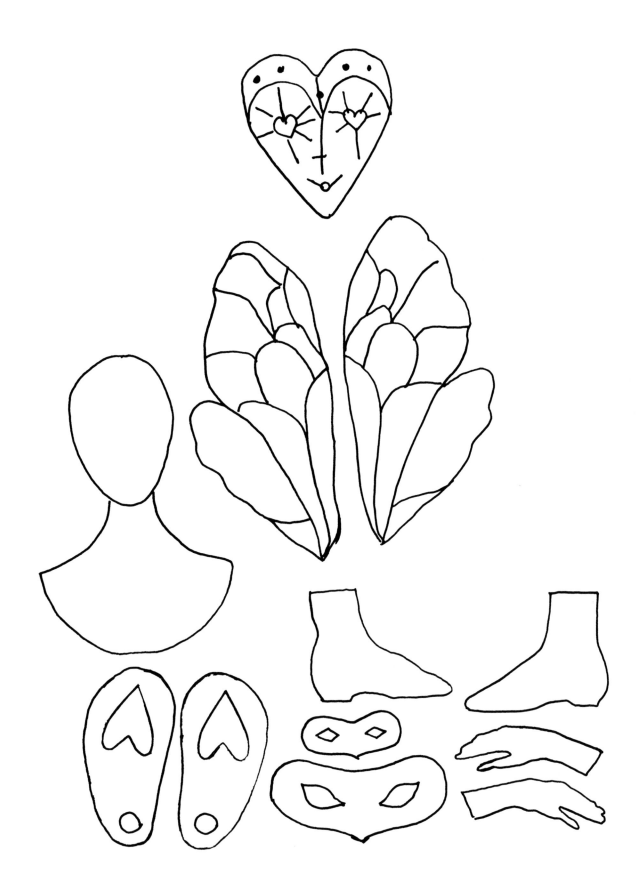

Patterns

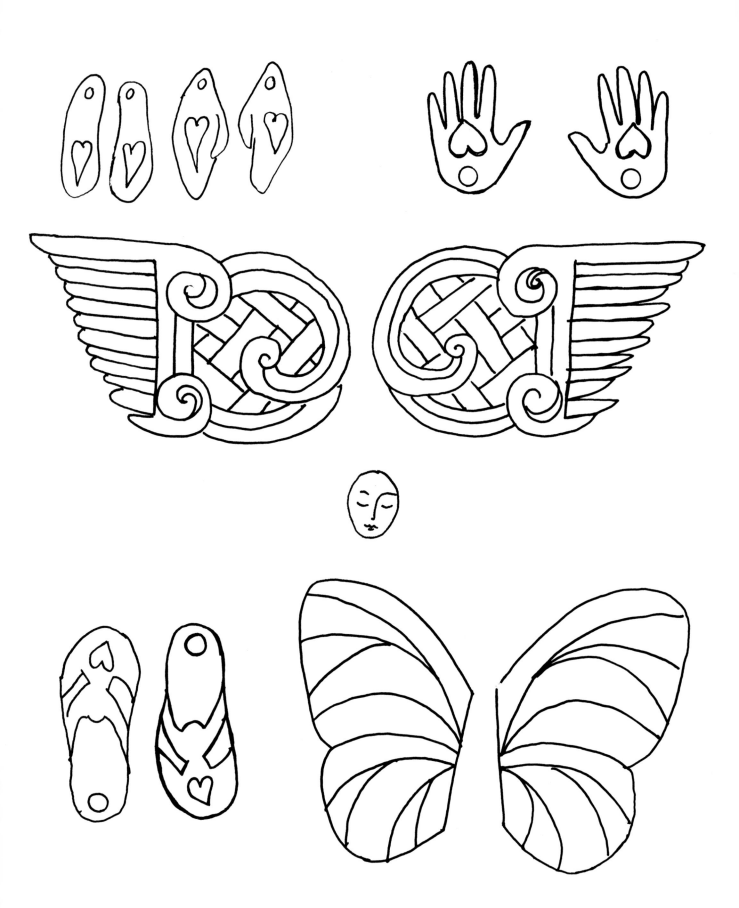

Patterns

Copper Foil Wings and Other Things

The copper foil in the photo came from Heritan. Copper foil is a wonderful medium for making wings, and even hearts or masks.

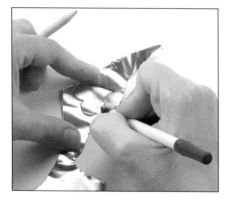

Instructions

1. Lay the copper foil onto a computer mouse pad or stack of paper.
2. Place the pattern on it.
3. Draw firmly with a ball-point pen or embossing tool.
4. Flip it over and stroke areas that you want to be raised.
5. Cut out with scissors or a craft knife.
6. To "antique" it, rub black or dark green acrylic paint on and buff off.
7. You may wish to glue wings to lightweight cardboard to stabilize them.

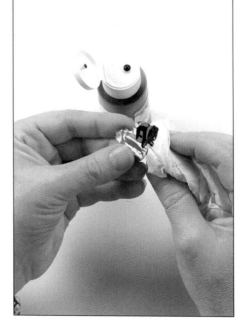

Crocheted Wings

The crocheted wings can be made in the same yarn or thread as the doll itself, or can be made in something else entirely. These two patterns for wings are used repeatedly throughout the book.

◀ Single Crochet Triangular Wings

The finished size of the wings depends on the size of hook and thickness of yarn you use.

Instructions

Begin: Make 2. Ch 8
Row 1: 1 sc in second ch from hook and in each remaining ch. (7 sc). Ch 1 and turn.
Row 2 - 4: 7 sc, ch 1, turn.
Row 5 - 8: Skip first sc, 1 sc in remaining sc, ch 1.
Row 9: Draw up a loop in each of the 3 remaining sc, yo, draw through all 4 loops on hook, ch 1. Sl st down side edge of wing to R 1, then cut yarn, leaving a 6" tail for stitching wing to doll. Pull end through loop.

▼ Noreen's Most Favorite Crocheted Wings

The cream-colored wings in the photo were crocheted with a 2mm hook using CGOA Presents Blithe #18. The size of the hook and weight of the yarn that you choose will determine the size of the wings. The wings are worked with both wings on a central ring.
Gauge: 7 rows and 7 sc = 1".

Instructions

Begin: Ch 7 for the ring. Join with a sl st.
First wing:
Row 1: Ch 4, 3 tr, ch 1, and turn.
Row 2: Work 1 sc and 1 hdc in the first tr; in next tr work: 1 dc, 1 tr, ch 4, sl st in 4th ch from hook, 1 dc; in last tr work: 1 hdc, 1 sc. Ch 5, sc in starting ring.
Second wing: Repeat first wing, then sl st in the sc in ring from the first wing.

Hair

Hair makes a huge statement on a doll. These methods are my favorites for adding hair to the dolls.

Ponytails or Tassels

Instructions

1. Cut a scrap of cardboard that is 2" wide. It doesn't matter how long it is.
2. Wrap two or more strands of yarn around the piece of cardboard several times. The number of strands that you use depends on the thickness of your yarn.
3. Snip one edge to open strands.
4. Fold strands in half.
5. Push hook (use a larger hook for this, perhaps one size bigger than the one you used to crochet the doll) through the side of the head and place the folded strands over it.
6. Pull through the stitch on the doll's head to form a loop.
7. Pull the ends through the loop.
8. Tug on ends to tighten it up.

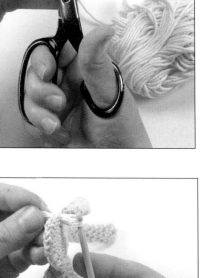

Wig with Tufts

Instructions

Wig Base: Ch 3, join to form ring. Ch 3, 11 dc in ring. Ch 1, cut yarn, pull end through last loop on hook.

Tufts: The tufts are made in exactly the same way as the ponytails. Cut a piece of cardboard that is 1½" wide, and wrap one or two strands of yarn (depending on the thickness of the yarn) around it 4 or 5 times for each tuft. Make one "mini-ponytail" in each dc of wig base.

Wig with Chained Loops

Instructions

Begin with the curls at top of the head: *Ch 10, join last ch to first*, repeat 3 times (3 curls made). Do not cut yarn.

Begin wig cap: Ch 4, join last ch to fourth ch from hook to form ring. Ch 3 (counts as first dc), 11 dc into ring (12 dc). Join the last dc to the first with a sl st.

Hair loops around edge of wig cap: Ch 10, join to first dc, *Ch 10, sc in next dc*.

Repeat from * to * 11 times. Cut yarn, pull end through last loop on hook.

Push the hook up through the center of the ch 4 ring of the wig cap and pull the starting yarn tail down through center. Tie a knot with it and the yarn end of the last hair loop.

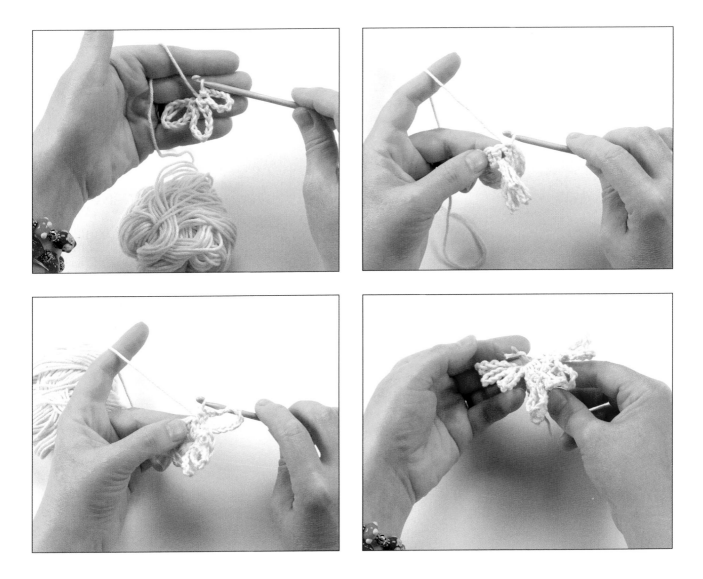

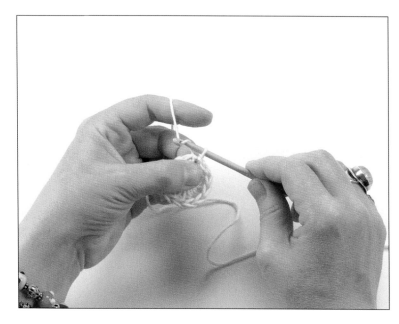

Wig with Yarn Loops

Instructions

Base of wig: Ch 3 (counts as a dc), join to form ring, ch 3, work 11 dc in ring. Join last dc to top of ch 3.

To make loops: Insert hook into top of dc, pull up a loop, yo.

Pull up a loop that is ½" long. Tug on it sharply to lock it.

Fold this loop over and hold on to it to keep it from getting pulled out, and work another loop in same stitch.

Continue all around the head, working 2 loops into each dc.

Glue or stitch to doll's head.

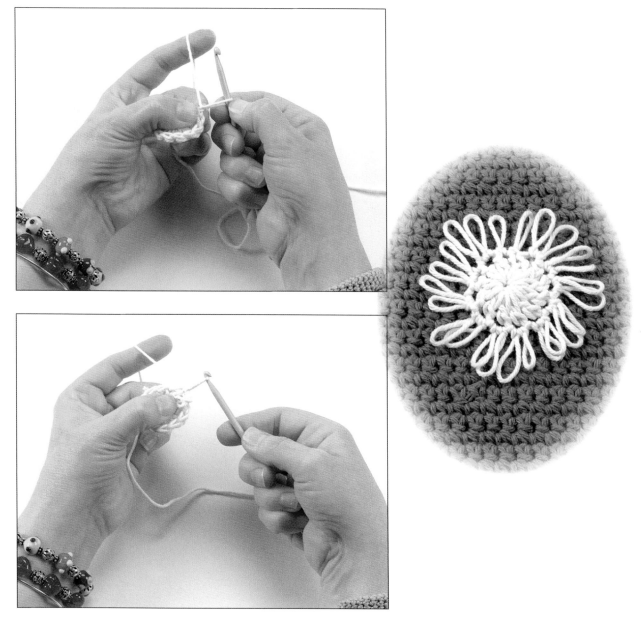

Crocheted Flower

I came up with this little chain stitch flower because I wanted a fast and simple little flower. You'll find it scattered throughout the book.

▼ Noreen's Chain Stitch Flower

Instructions

Begin: Ch 5, join last ch to first. * ch 5, 1 sc in ring * 5 times. This makes the inner round of petals, but can also be used, as is, as a small flower.

For a larger flower: Work a second row of petals by* ch 7, 1 sc in next sc * 5 times. Ch 1, cut yarn, pull end through last loop on hook. *(Note: For a flower with three tiers of petals, work another round with 9 ch per petal.)*

Leaves: Join leaf color to yarn or thread end.
Ch 4. 2 dc in 4th ch from hook, ch 4, join to the base of the leaf. *Ch 7, go behind two petals and work 1 sc in sc of flower and work another leaf* twice. Ch 5, join to starting sc. Ch 1, cut yarn end, tie a small knot to green yarn. Trim ends.

Butterflies

I wanted a simple little butterfly that would be the right size for the dolls, and so I designed this one. I just love it! You can make it all one color, or you can use different colors for the body and wings. When you fold this butterfly in half, and stitch the edges together, it makes a wonderful shoe.

▲Noreen's Butterfly

Instructions

Body: Ch 8 with body color, 1 dc in 5th ch from hook, 1 dc in each remaining ch.
The butterfly body is these 4 dc, and the turning ch, which is the equivalent of 5 dc.
If you are changing colors for the wings, cut body color and join wing color.
First upper wing: Ch 7, form a picot by sl st in the 4th ch from hook, 2 tr in first dc, 2 dc in 2nd dc, 1 hdc and 1 sc in 3rd dc.
First lower wing: 1 sc in 4th dc, 1 hdc and 2 dc in top ch of turning ch, ch 3, sl st in same ch right beside the second dc in this stitch. Ch 3, skip 2 ch of the end of the lower body; join with a sl st to next ch.
Second lower wing: Working along the starting ch of the body: Ch 3, 2 dc and 1 hdc in same st (fifth st from starting knot).
Second upper wing: 1 sc in one loop of next ch, 1 sc and 1 hdc in next ch, 2 dc in next ch, 2 tr in last ch, make picot: Ch 4, sl st in fourth ch from hook. Ch 4, join to starting st. Cut yarn, pull end through last loop on hook. Weave in ends.

Lace Shawl

Another fun way to use the flowers and butterflies is to make a random lace shawl. "Random Lace" is the term that I came up with to describe the technique of making these shawls.

◀ Random Lace Shawl

Instructions

1. Cut out the shawl shape in heavy brown paper or cloth.
2. Crochet a bunch of flowers and butterflies and pin them to the shawl shape. Place the pins on the back of the paper so they don't get in the way.

3. Attach fine crochet or tatting cotton to one of the flowers and chain 7 or 9 or so, and sc to another petal or leaf of the flower.
4. Continue to work chain loops around the flower until you are within "chaining distance" of another motif. Chain loop to it and around it. Continue until you have captured all the motifs, and have worked chain loops to fill the shape of the shawl. You will need to pin the corner loops to the pattern.

Covered Rings

Cabone rings are nifty little items. When covered with single crochet, they can be used as design elements in the doll, or you can sew one to the back of the doll and hang her on the wall. Plastic cabone rings are covered with sc in exactly the same way as the brim of the hat on pages 126 and 127.

center fold

Cut one on fold

Shawl Shape

chapter two

Basic Dolls

Let's begin with what I call "The Basic Doll." I have been working with this simple little doll pattern for many years, and am delighted by the endless variations and possibilities that it offers. I love it because it is a fairly accurate representation of the human figure but, at the same time, it is also somewhat abstract. Because this book is an exploration of creativity, I have documented how I worked with this doll, and how it ignited my imagination and became the guide to a wonderful voyage of discovery!

The Basic Doll Pattern

All the dolls in this book have sprung from this Basic Doll pattern. There are a couple of ways to make the Basic Doll. The size of the finished doll is determined by the thickness of the yarn and the size of the hook that you use. Finished height of doll: approximately 4¼" tall. Gauge: 7 sc and 8 rows = 1". Below, you'll find a materials list for what you'll need to make the Basic Doll.

◀ Pattern #1: Basic Doll

Worked Flat then Sewn

Instructions

Begin:
At the tip of the toes on leg #1: Ch 4.
Row 1: 1 sc in 2nd ch from hook, 1 sc in remaining 2 ch. Ch 1 and turn (3 sc).
Row 2: 2 sc in first 2 sc of previous row, 3 sc in last sc. Ch 1 and turn (7 sc).
Rows 3 - 15: 1 sc in each sc, ch 1 and turn. At end of R 15, cut yarn and pull end through last loop. Leave a yarn end that is 6" long for sewing.

Leg #2:

Repeat R 1 - 15, but at the end of Row 15, do not cut yarn.

Body:

Row 16: Work 1 sc in each of 7 sc of second leg, then work 1 sc in each of 7 sc of first leg (14 sc). Ch 1 and turn.
Rows 17 - 24: Work 14 sc, ch 1 and turn.

Materials

- 2.5mm hook
- Yarn, CGOA Presents: Blithe #18
- Scissors
- Darning needle

What goes into the making of your doll? Hopefully, you put love and delight in every stitch. What goes inside your doll? Many different things can go into your doll:

The fabric that you create when crocheting the doll may be dense enough to not require stuffing. For example, a doll that is going to have a pin sewn to her back may be better left unstuffed. But a doll that is going to be played with or needs to be supported for standing on a shelf might need to be stuffed. A doll that is intended to be displayed in a sitting position is better without stuffing in the legs. The arms will not need stuffing.

You can write poems, prayers, blessings, benedictions, good wishes or thoughts on paper or fabric, roll them up, and insert them in the doll instead of, or as well as, the "usual" stuffing (polyester fiberfill). Inside every single doll in this book there is some kind of blessing, benediction, or prayer written on paper or fabric.

Row 25: *Draw up a loop in each of the next 2 sc, yo, pull through all three loops on hook*. Repeat from * to * 7 times (7 sc); ch 1 and turn.

Rows 26 - 27: Work 7 sc, ch 1 and turn.

Row 28: Inc by working 2 sc in each sc (14 sc). Ch 1 and turn.

Rows 29 - 31: Work 14 sc, ch 1 and turn.

Row 32: Repeat from * to * 7 times (7 sc) ch 1 and turn.

Row 33: Repeat from * to * 3 times, 1 sc in last sc (4 sc) ch 1, cut yarn, leaving a 9" long tail for stitching doll.

Arms:

Make 2. Ch 4.

Row 1: 1 sc in 2nd ch from hook, 1 sc in remaining 2 ch. Ch 1 and turn (3 sc).

Row 2: 2 sc in each sc of previous row. Ch 1 and turn (6 sc).

Rows 3 - 11: 1 sc in each of 6 sc. Ch 1 and turn.

Row 12: Repeat from * to * 3 times (3 sc). Ch 1. Cut yarn, leaving a 6" long tail for stitching, and pull end through last loop on hook.

Assembling Doll

1. Fold edges of first leg together and sew seam using the yarn end. Stitch from hip to toe, being sure to anchor yarn firmly at toe. Take yarn inside leg.

2. Beginning at top of head, stitch back seam of body closed, and then down one leg inseam. Then, stitch remaining leg inseam shut.

Note: See Sidebar about stuffing the doll.

Pattern #2: Basic Doll

Worked in the Round

Instructions

Begin: At tip of toes: Leg #1: ch 3, join to form ring, ch 1.

Row 1: 7 sc in ring, join last sc to first with a sl st then ch 1.

Rows 2 - 15: 7 sc in round, join, ch 1. At end of R 15, cut yarn, pull end through last loop on hook. Take yarn end inside leg.

Second Leg:

Repeat R 1 - 15 of Leg #1, but at the end of R 15, do not cut yarn.

Body:

Row 16: Worked over both legs. Work 7 sc on second leg, do not join last sc to first, but continue working 1 sc in each sc of last round of first leg. Join last sc to first sc and ch 1 (14 sc).

Rows 17 - 24: 14 sc in each round, join, ch 1.

Row 25: *Draw up a loop in each of the next 2 sc, yo, pull through all 3 loops on hook* repeat from * to *, join, ch 1 (7 sc).

Rows 26 - 27: 7 sc in each round, join, ch 1.

Row 28: 2 sc in each sc of previous round, join, ch 1 (14 sc).

Rows 29 - 31: 14 sc in each round, join, ch 1.

Row 32: Repeat from * to * 7 times join, ch 1 (7 sc).

Row 33: Repeat from * to * 3 times, 1 sc in remaining sc, join, ch 1 (4 sc). Cut yarn, pull end through loop. Stitch top of head shut if necessary. Take end inside doll.

Profile Face Basic Doll
◀ Version # 1: Working in the Round

I love the Basic Doll with her forward-looking face, but I wondered if her face could be crocheted in profile. Well, of course it could! But I wanted to be able to crochet the face in profile while working in the round—good heavens, that took a lot of counting, crocheting, and unraveling! Ah well, I am quite pleased with the results. Even so, there are also times when it would be easier to just do a graph and work the doll flat and sew up the outside edge of the doll.

Crocheting the Profile Face in a continuous spiraling round can be a little challenging, but is worth it. After you finish crocheting it, tug at the tip of the nose and chin vigorously to persuade them into shape.

Instructions

Begin at Round 27 of the "Basic Doll in the Round" pattern: 7 sc, do not join. Ch 3 for the chin. 1 sc in next 7 sc. 3 sc in the chin ch 3 space. 1 sc in next 19 sc. Ch 3 for the nose. 1 sc in next 10 sc. 3 sc in the nose 3 ch space.
1 sc in each of next 11 sc. Draw up a loop in each of the next 3 sc, yo, pull yarn through all 4 loops on hook.
1 sc in next 15 sc. (Draw up a loop in each of next 2 sc, yo, pull yarn through all 3 loops on hook) 7 times.

Cut yarn and thread into darning needle, then gather stitches of last round.
Take yarn end inside head.

Note: To work just a Profile Face on its own: Ch 7, join, ch 1, work 3 rounds of 7 sc, join, ch 1, for the neck and then work the head.

Profile Face Basic Doll

Version #2: Working Flat from a Graph ▶

Instructions

Begin: Work 2 sections in sc.
Note: At Row 14, the chin, you will sc in the second ch from the hook to make the chin. This is really important for shaping the chin; it gives a more definite chin line than working 2 sc in the same stitch.

Nose:

At the end of Row 15, chain 3. To shape the nose, on Row 16, you form the nose by making a picot—work a sc in the third ch from the hook. At the end of Row 17, draw up a loop in each of the 5th sc and the picot, yo, draw through all three loops on hook.

Top of Head:

Draw up a loop in each of 3 sc in Row 18.
When stitching the face sections together, take tiny stitches, close together, especially when shaping the nose.

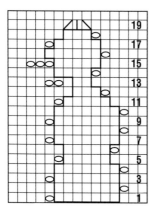

chapter three

Lots of Dolls:

Fanciful Fairies,

Adorable Babies,

and

Assorted Critters

A Creative Figure

Since this is a book about creativity, it makes sense to me to begin with an homage to Albert Einstein. We'll be using the Basic Doll pattern, but will be tweaking it ever so slightly to make it bend in the direction of Albert Einstein.

An Homage to Albert Einstein

Gauge: 4 sc and 4 rows = 1".

Instructions

Begin : Make doll following Basic Doll pattern on page 44 or 45, but work 5 extra rounds in blue for shoes, 15 rounds of leg in green, the first three rows of the body in green, 6 rounds in burgundy and remaining rounds of neck and head in beige.

Arms: Work 3 rounds beige, 9 rounds burgundy. Stuff legs and body just before you make the decreases for the neck. Stuff the head just before you decrease at the top of the head. Stuff arms after crocheting.

Make wig with tufts following instructions on page 35.

Sew wig to doll's head.

Nose: Lay the end of the crochet hook on the center of the face and stitch over and over it in one place to form the nose.

Eyes: Stitch a black "e" bead on either side of nose for eyes.

Eyebrows: Embroider a couple of straight stitches over each eye for eyebrow.

Mustache: Lay a size J, 6mm crochet hook, right under nose, and stitch over and over it to make mustache.

Fold the feet up and stitch them in place.

Make the heart out of paper or wood veneer, and paint or burn "E=mc^2" on it. Then glue it to chest.

Materials

- 3.5mm (E) hook
- Yarn, CGOA Presents:
  Kid Mohair #01 White for hair
  Chenille #557 Blue for the shoes
  Chenille #324 Burgundy for sweater
  Chenille #217 Green
  Celebrity #14 White Linen (2 strands held together)
- Small amount of polyester stuffing
- Darning needle
- Small amount of stuffing
- 2 black "e" beads for eyes

Exploring Themes and Variations

Remember that when you use different sizes of hooks and different thicknesses of threads or yarns, you will end up with different sizes of dolls.

I made the largest doll in the photo with Lily Sugar 'n Cream #01 White, and a size "H" 5mm hook, which gave a gauge of 7 sc and 7 rows = 2". She's 9" tall. I crocheted the flower on her chest with embroidery floss and a 1.5mm hook. See page 38 for instructions. She wears Celtic wings, burned onto wood veneer (wooden business cards from Lee Valley). See page 32 for pattern. The doll with the rainbow heart (punched from a photo) and a flower for a hat was crocheted with Patons Grace and a 2.5mm hook, which gave a gauge of 5 sc and 5 rows = 1". She's 5" tall. Her wings are the Butterfly wings on page 32. They are also wood veneer, which has been burned with a wood-burning tool. The small doll was crocheted with #8 Perle cotton and a 1mm hook. This gave a gauge of 12 sc and 12 rows = 1". She's 2¾" tall. I crocheted the tiniest doll with #50 crochet cotton and a .5mm hook gauge is 14 sc and 14 rows = 1". She's 2⅛" tall. She and her slightly taller sister both have brass charm hearts from Fancifuls Inc. Their wings are the "Favorite Wing" pattern on page 34.

Made with the Basic Pattern

The Dragonfly Fairy ▶

I made the Fairy with the orange hair with two strands of CGOA Presents Blithe #02 Black, held together and crocheted with a 3.25mm (D) hook. She is 6½" tall; 5 sc and 5 rows = 1". Her wings are made of paper. See page 31 for the pattern. The flower on her chest was made with CGOA Presents Splendor #05 and a 2.5mm hook. Here's the drawing for her face.

◀ The Art Nouveau Fairy

This fairy has copper wings (pattern page 32) and a brass charm face. She was made with a 1.75mm hook and CGOA Presents Celebrity Dark Teal. Work her in spirals (continuously worked rows that are not joined at the end of each row). Each sc was worked only in the back horizontal bar of the sc of the previous row. The arms were worked as one unit of 6 sc for 22 rows and then sewn to the shoulders, after the charm was glued to her head. Her skirt is made of three sections that were crocheted following the triangle wings on page 34. They are gathered and stitched or glued to her hips. She has a pin glued to her back so that she can be worn as a pin doll.

More Fairies
Made with the Profile Pattern

The profile fairies were crocheted following the chart on page 53. Their teakettle and watering can are copper ornaments from Lee Valley. Their wings are wooden, burned with a wood burning tool. See page 32. Their hats are made by crocheting two of Noreen's Little Butterflies for each hat (see page 39), and gluing them to the doll's heads. Their shoes are made by splitting the yarn and crocheting butterflies with the thinner yarn and smaller hook. Their hands are also made with the split, thinner yarn and smaller hooks. See page 28 for pattern.

◀ The Purple Fairy

The Purple Fairy is crocheted with Lily Sugar 'n Cream Plum, Grape, and Cream and a 4mm hook.

She is approximately 10½" tall. 7 sc and 10 rows = 2". The feet, hands, and collar are all made with just two of the four strands of the yarn. Cut lengths of yarn that are about 2 yards long then divide the four strands into two strands. Wrap the split yarn around your pointer and baby finger in a figure eight to keep it from tangling. Work the split yarn with a 2.5mm hook. The collar is made up of four sections, each of which is the Triangle Wing on page 34. Use the chart so that contrasting colors always line up with each other.

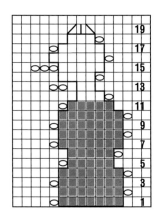

The Pink Fairy ▶

The Pink Fairy is crocheted with Patons Bumble Bee Flowers Variegated and Patons Grace Natural with a 4mm hook. She is approximately 8½" tall. 8 sc and 10 rows = 2". The feet and hands are made with just one of the three strands of the yarn. Cut lengths of yarn that are about 2 yards long then divide the three strands into single strands. Wrap the split yarn around your pointer and baby finger in a figure eight to keep it from tangling. Work the split yarn with a 2mm hook. The skirt is made up of four sections, each of which is the Triangle Wing on page 34. Use the chart with variegated yarn; from row 12 to row 19 use flesh-colored yarn. The flower on her chest was crocheted with Perle cotton and a 1.5mm hook.

The Flying Fairy ▼

The Flying Fairy is crocheted with fine hemp from Heritan. Her wings are made with copper foil, which has been glued to mat board to stabilize it. And they've been antiqued by rubbing black acrylic paint on and then buffing it off. The pattern is on page 32. The doll is crocheted in spirals, without joining at the end of the row. The sc are worked into the back horizontal bar of the sc in the previous row. Her wig is the chain loop wig on page 36. She was crocheted with a 2.5mm hook which gave a gauge of 5 sc and 5 rows= 1". She is 4" high and about 8" long. There is a loop of cord glued between the wings to so she can fly!

The Blue Fairy ▲

The Blue Fairy is a different kind of Profile Doll, because her charm face is in profile! She is the Basic Doll pattern crocheted with cotton quilting fabric that was cut into ¼" wide strips. She was crocheted with a size G or 4mm hook. This doll is 10" tall. 4 sc and 4 rows = 1". Her face, hands, heart, wings, and shoes are all brass charms from Fanciful Inc. Her skirt is the triangle wing (see page 34 for instructions), crocheted three times.

Starbabies

I once had a delightful dream in which the Northern Lights touched down in our garden. All kinds of wildly laughing little Starbabies slid down the Northern Lights, as if they were a water slide. What a great dream! I've been making Starbaby dolls ever since. The silver Starbaby has a brass charm star face from Fancifuls Inc. They were both crocheted with CGOA Presents Sparkle (Silver and Moonbeams) with a 3.5mm hook. They are approximately 5½" tall.

◀ The Rainbow Doll

Yarn: Lily Sugar 'n Cream Rainbow Bright. Hook: G, 4mm. Gauge: 4 sc and 4 rows = 1". Finished size: 8" not including her hair. She has an embroidered heart (see Instructions on page 27), with a vintage heart-shaped bead sewn in the center. The face is an embroidered and painted paper heart (page 31). The nose and mouth are "e" beads. Her wings are the simple crocheted Triangle Wings. The instructions to make her hair are below.

Instructions

1. Cut 4 strands of cotton, each 4" long.
2. Pull the ends through a stitch at the side of her head with a crochet hook.
3. Pull ends through a pony bead (use a smaller crochet hook) then, push bead against the head and apply a dab of glue to secure.

◀ Roving Doll

This soft doll was crocheted with unspun mohair roving (from the Fleece Artist). I separated the roving into strands that were about a ¼" wide and crocheted them with a 7mm hook. This gave me a gauge of 3 sc and 3 rows = 1". She's about 12" tall. Her face is a crocheted and embroidered heart (see page 26). She wears a Random Lace Shawl (see page 40). Her cherub broach, hands, and shoes are brass charms, painted with nail polish and acrylics.

Some Charming Critters ▼

The charms for these critters all came from Fancifuls Inc. The Elephant was made with CGOA Presents Splendor 02 and a 2.5mm hook. Her wings are actually glasses. She is about 4" tall. The Giraffe was made with CGOA Presents Celebrity #12 and #18 held together, with a 3.5mm hook. She's about 6½" tall.

The Rooster was made with CGOA Presents Sparkle Gold and a 3.5mm hook. His wings are the Favorite Wings Pattern on page 34, crocheted with a 5mm hook and unspun roving from Fleece Artist. He's about 6" tall.

Cats with Faces ▶

You can make these cats with brass charms (the charm in the photo is from Fancifuls Inc), or paper or wooden faces. (See Instructions on page 29.) Finished height of cat: Approximately 6½". Gauge: 5 sc and 5 rows = 1". The Wooden-faced Cat was crocheted with yarn that I handspun.

Instructions

Row 1 - 3: Work the legs with two strands of white yarn held together.

Rows 4 - 33: Work with 1 strand white kid mohair held together with the 2 brown yarns. Do not increase to 14 sc on R 28. Head is worked on 7 sc only.

Rows 1 - 3: To make the arms, work the legs with 2 strands of white yarn held together.

Rows 4 - 12: Work with l strand white kid mohair held together with the two brown yarns.

Bib: With white.

Row 1: Ch 8, 1 sc in 2nd ch from hook, 1 sc in each ch to end of ch. (7 sc).

Rows 2 - 3: Skip first sc, 1 sc in each sc to last 2 sc, dec over last 2 sc, ch 1 and turn.

Row 4: Draw up a loop in each of the 3 sc, yo, pull through all 4 loops on hook. Ch 1, cut yarn, pull end through loop.

Tail: With white, ch 3, join, ch 1.

Row 1: 4 sc in ring, join, ch 1.

Rows 2 - 3: 4 sc in white, ch 1. Cut yarn, join brown yarn.

Rows 4 - 11: 4 sc in brown yarn ch 1.

Cut yarn, leaving 5" for stitching. Sew tail to cat's bottom.

Patch for the back of the head: Ch 3, join to form ring. Ch 3, 11 dc in ring, join last dc to top of ch 3. Do not join.

Finishing

1. Sew arms to cat's body.

2. Sew tail to cat's bottom.

3. Sew bib to cat's chest.

4. Glue face to front of head.

5. Glue back of head patch to the back of the cat's head, pushing the corners of the starting ch 3 and last dc into the Cat's ears.

Materials

- 3.75mm (F) hook
- Yarn, CGOA Presents:
  White Kid Mohair #01
  Frolic #01
  Graceful #09
  Splendor #05
- Fabric glue
- Darning needle
- Brass charm from Fancifuls Inc., or wooden or paper face

◀ Rabbit with Paper or Wooden Face

It was the oddest thing! I kept trying and trying to draw a rabbit face, but every single one looked astonishingly fierce—not at all what I had in mind. So, I gave up and drew this very goofy one. It made me laugh, so there you have it! The vest is made following the pattern for the Pocket Doll's vest on page 66 with one strand each of #11 and #10 mohair from CGOA Presents, held together while working, and a 3.5mm hook. Finished height of rabbit: Approximately 8". Gauge: 5 sc and 5 rows = 1".

Instructions

1. The rabbit is made following Basic Doll Pattern on pages 44 and 45.
2. Make head, hands, and feet from paper or wood veneer and color or burn details.
3. The face is then glued to the front of the head.
4. Pierce or burn a hole in hands and feet and take yarn through hole.
5. Glue into ends of arms and legs.
6. Make a tail in the same way as the Little Bunny's tail on page 60.

Materials

- 3.5mm hook
- Yarn (2 strands held together), CGOA Presents: Kid Mohair #01
- Fabric glue
- Darning needle
- Wood veneer or old business cards or watercolor paper glued to card stock to stiffen it
- A wood-burning tool if you are using wood veneer

Zebra ▶

Finished height of Zebra: Approximately 6" (not including mane). Gauge: 6 sc and 6 rows = 1".

Instructions

1. Holding both strands together, make arms, legs, and body following Basic Doll pattern on pages 44 and 45. Do not work increases on Row 28. Work Rows 28 - 31 on 7 sc.
2. To make mane: Make six tufts up the side of neck/head, just like the ones in the Instructions for the Wig with Tufts (page 35).
3. Glue charm to neck/head, pushing it into the charm.
4. *Tail:* Holding two strands dark and two strands light together, ch 5. Cut yarn end, pull through last loop on hook. Stitch to zebra's bottom.
5. *Hooves:* Run a bead of glue for 1/2" at wrists and ankles. Wrap with black yarn. Push ends into glue.

Materials

- 3.5mm (E) hook
- Brass charms from Fancifuls Inc.
- Yarn, CGOA Presents:
  Blithe #02 Black
  Blithe #13 Natural
- Fabric glue

Cuddly Critters

Basic Teddy Bear ▼

Finished height of Teddy Bear: Approximately 3". Gauge: 9 sc and 9 rows = 1".

Materials

- 1.75mm hook
- Yarn, CGOA Presents: Celebrity #12
- Black embroidery floss or yarn to embroider eyes, nose, and mouth
- Small amount of stuffing
- Embroidery or darning needle
- Paper clip and needle-nose pliers to make glasses

Instructions

Make Basic Teddy Bear following Basic Doll pattern on pages 44 and 45. At top of head, do not cut yarn.

Ear:

Work 5 dc in 2nd round from hook. Then, attach ear to head by working 1 sc two rows down from starting point. Cut yarn, pull through last loop on hook, then take yarn end inside head.

Rejoin yarn at top of head and work 2nd ear in the same way as the first.

Muzzle:

R1: Ch 3, join to form ring, ch 1, then work 7 sc in the ring, join, ch 1.

R2: 1 sc in each sc of previous round, join, ch 1 (7 sc). Cut yarn, pull end through last loop on hook.

Stuff muzzle and sew to face.

Embroider dots for eyes (or stitch on beads), and nose and mouth, following diagram.

Fold feet up and stitch in place.

Make glasses (see instructions page 18). Push ends through base of ears, curl ends down then clip off extra wire.

◀ Little Bunny

Finished height of Little Bunny: Approximately 5" including ears. Gauge: 7 sc and 7 rows = 1".

Instructions

Make Little Bunny following the Basic Doll pattern on pages 44 and 45. At top of head, do not cut yarn.

Ear: Ch 1, R 1, work 2 sc at side of top of head, ch 1, turn.

Row 2: 2 sc in each sc of previous row, ch 1 (4 sc).

Rows 3 - 5: 4 sc, ch 1, turn.

Row 6: Draw up a loop in all 4 sc, yo, pull yarn through all 5 loops on hook, ch 1, sl st down the inside edge of the ear to the top of the head.

Second ear: Repeat Rows 1 - 6. At end of second ear, sl st down to center top of head, cut yarn, draw end through last loop on hook.

Rub blusher on the inside of the ears.

Fold feet up and stitch in place.

Bunny tail: Anchor yarn by making a couple of tiny stitches in one place on bunny's bottom. Hold the end of a crochet hook on bunny's bottom. Sew over and over nine times. Pull out the hook. Anchor stitches again. Cut yarn, and take inside bunny.

Bunny Materials

- 2.5mm hook
- Yarn (two strands), CGOA Presents: Kid Mohair #01
- Darning needle
- Blusher for inside ears
- A pencil for making tail

Kitten Materials

- 2.5mm hook
- Yarn, CGOA Presents: Kid Mohair #11
- Darning needle

▲ Little Kitten

Finished height of Little Kitten: Approximately 4½" tall including ears. Gauge: 7 sc and 7 rows = 1".

Instructions

Make Little Kitten following Basic Doll pattern on pages 44 and 45. At top of head, do not cut yarn.

Ear: Ch 1.

Row 1: Work 2 sc at side of top of head, ch 1, turn.

Row 2: 1 sc in each sc of previous row, ch 1 (2 sc).

Row 3: Draw up a loop in both sc, yo, pull yarn through all three loops on hook, ch 1, sl st down the inside edge of the ear to the top of the head.

Second ear: Repeat Rows 1 - 3. At end of second ear, sl st down to center top of head, cut yarn, draw end through last loop on hook.

Fold feet up and stitch in place.

Kitty tail: Join yarn by making a couple of tiny stitches in one place on kitty's bottom. Take hook into a stitch, yo, then pull up a loop and ch 10. 1 sc in 2nd ch from hook and in each remaining ch (9 sc). Cut yarn, pull end through last loop on hook. Thread end into darning needle and stitch in place a couple of times, then take inside kitten.

Little Girl in a Hat ▶

The Little Girl in a Hat has a face that was made by tracing a dime onto cardstock, and then drawing and coloring the face. Or, you could cut out a photocopy of a favorite photo and glue it to her head for the face. Her hair is a tuft of roving from the Fleece Artist. Her hat is crocheted with embroidery floss and a 1.5mm hook, following the pattern on page 69. Her heart was punched out of a photograph. Her wings are charms from Fanciful Inc. Her skirt is the triangle wing (see page 34), crocheted four times with a single strand and a 3.5mm hook. They were gathered onto a strand of yarn and then tied around her waist.

Little Girl with Ponytails ▶

The doll in the photograph was made with a 2mm hook and CGOA Presents Splendor #4 for the body, arms, legs, and skirt. Her hair was made with CGOA Presents Kid Mohair (1 strand #18 and 1 strand #17 held together). Her face was made with CGOA Presents Tropic #14. There is a small amount of polyester stuffing in her body and head. She has a paper heart glued to her chest and purple ⅜" diameter domed buttons for shoes. The doll in the photograph is approximately 4½" tall. The gauge is: 8 sc and 8 rows = 1". Feel free to use the yarn and appropriate hook of your choice.

Instructions

Follow the Basic Doll pattern on pages 44 and 45, using variegated yarn for arms, and the legs and body from Rows 1 - 27.
After completing Row 27, cut yarn and join mohair.
Stuff the body at this point (see sidebar on Stuffing, page 44).
Work head in mohair for Rows 28 - 33.
Face: With skin-tone yarn, ch 4.
Row 1: 1 sc in 2nd ch from hook and remaining ch (3 sc). Ch 1, turn.
Row 2: 2 sc in first sc, 1 sc in next sc, 2 sc in last sc (5 sc). Ch 1, turn.
Rows 3 - 4: 5 sc, ch 1, turn.
R 5: Draw up a loop in each of the first 2 sc, yo, pull through all 3 loops on hook, 1 sc in next sc, draw up a loop in each of the last 2 sc, yo, pull through all 3 loops on hook, (3 sc) ch 1, cut yarn, leaving a 6" tail for stitching and pull through last loop on hook.
Skirt: With variegated yarn, ch 14. Join to form ring. Ch 4, then work 29 tr into ring. Join last tr to top of ch 4. Cut yarn, leaving a 6" tail for stitching and pull through last loop on hook. Thread it onto a darning needle and weave the end into skirt, through the ch 4, and then sew it to the doll just below her waist.

Finishing

1. Sew face to head.
2. **Hair:** Made with two strands of mohair, following instructions on page 35.
3. Make glasses from a paper clip (see instructions on page 18) and glue to face.
4. Stitch buttons to front of legs at ends, to make the shoes.
5. Make heart from a paper clip or wire, and glue or sew to chest, pushing ends of wire into chest. Or you could sew a button or a charm to her chest.

The Pocket Dolly and Her Wardrobe

The skirt on the doll with pink ponytails (page 61) made me think, "What about making changeable clothes for the doll?" And that was how I conjured up this doll and her clothes! The Pocket Dolly wearing yellow was crocheted with a 2.5mm hook. Her skin tone is CGOA Presents Frolic #4. Her undies are CGOA Presents Frolic #17. Her hair is CGOA Presents Kid Mohair #15 (two strands held together while working). Her glasses are charms from Fancifuls Inc. (#3543). The Pocket Dolly wearing stripes was crocheted with a 2.5mm hook. Her skin tone is CGOA Presents Blithe #20. Her undies are CGOA Presents Splendor #4 and #3. Her hair is CGOA Presents Kid Mohair #18 (two strands held together while working). Her shoes are CGOA Presents Blithe #3 Red (worked for three rows, then legs are worked in skin tone for the rest of the rows). Gauge: 7 sc and 7 rows = 1". Finished height of the Pocket Dollies: Approximately 4½". The Pocket Dollies were made following the Basic Doll pattern. To make their wigs: See instructions for yarn loop wigs on page 37.

The Clothing

Note: Be sure to make the clothing out of the same kind of yarn as the doll, using the same hook. If it is a different kind of yarn, then be sure the gauge is exactly the same as the gauge for the body.

◀ Drawstring Pants

Finished size: Approximately 2½" high. Gauge: 7 sc and 7 rows = 1".

Instructions

Beginning at cuff of leg: Ch 11 loosely, join to form ring, ch 1. Make 2.

Rows 1 - 12: 11 sc, join, ch 1. After Row 12 of first leg, cut yarn and pull end through last loop.

Row 13: For the second leg, work 11 sc; do not join. Work 11 sc of first leg (22 sc). Join last sc to first, ch 1.

Rows 14 - 15: 22 sc, join, ch 1.

Row 16: 22 sc, join, ch 4.

Row 17: Skip first sc, * 1 dc in next sc, ch 1 * repeat from * to * to end of round, join last ch to 3rd ch of ch 4. Cut yarn, thread into needle, weave back through the three vertical ch to hide yarn end in body of pants.

For the belt, with two strands held together: Ch 30. Cut yarn, pull end through last loop on hook. Weave in and out of ch 1 spaces, starting and ending at center front.

Materials

- 2.5mm hook
- Yarn, CGOA Presents: Frolic #11

◀ Sleeveless Top

Finished size: Approximately 1¾" high by 1½" wide. Gauge: 7 sc and 7 rows = 1".

Instructions

The Sleeveless Top is worked from side to side. Beginning at one side of back: ch 9.

Row 1: 1 sc in 2nd ch from hook and in each remaining ch (8 sc). Ch 1 and turn.

Row 2: 1 sc in each of the 8 sc, ch 5 and turn.

Row 3: 1 sc in 2nd ch from hook, 1 sc in next 4 ch, 1 sc in next 8 sc (12 sc). Ch 1 and turn.

Row 4: 1 sc in each of 10 sc, ch 1 and turn.

Row 5 - 7: 10 sc, ch 1 and turn.

Row 8: 10 sc, ch 3 and turn.

Row 9: 1 sc in 2nd ch from hook, 1 sc in next ch, 10 sc, (12 sc) ch 1 and turn.

Rows 10 - 11: 8 sc, ch 1 and turn. Cut yarn, leaving a 6" tail for sewing, pull through last loop on hook.

Front: Beginning at one side of top, ch 9.

Row 1: 1 sc in 2nd ch from hook and in each remaining ch. (8 sc) ch 1 and turn.

Row 2: 8 sc, ch 4, now, to join front section to back section: Take hook out of loop, insert hook in one shoulder stitch of the back section, pick up and pull loop from the front section of the top through the stitch from the back (join is now complete).

Row 3: Ch 1 and work 1 sc in each of the 4 ch, then 1 sc in each remaining sc, ch 1 and turn.

Row 4: 1 sc in each of 10 sc, ch 1 and turn.

Row 5 - 7: 10 sc, ch 1 and turn.

Row 8: 10 sc, ch 2, take loop off hook, hook goes through the other shoulder st of the back. Pick up the loop from the front section and take this loop through the back section loop. Join second shoulder. Ch 1.

Row 9: 1 sc in each of 2 ch, 1 sc in each remaining sc (12 sc).

Rows 10 - 11: 8 sc, ch 1 and turn.

Cut yarn, leaving a 6" tail for sewing, pull through last loop on hook. Sew side seams and weave in ends.

Materials

- 2.5mm hook
- Yarn, CGOA Presents: Splendor #4

◀ Pullover Sweater

Finished size: Approximately 1¾" high by 3½" wide. Gauge: 7 sc and 7 rows = 1".

Instructions

Make body of sweater following instructions for Sleeveless Top.

Sleeves: Make 2. Ch 10, join, ch 1.

Row 1: Work 10 sc in ring, join, ch 1.

Rows 2 - 10: 10 sc, join, ch 1.

After last round, cut yarn, leaving 6" tail for sewing. Stitch sleeves into armholes. Weave in ends.

Materials

- 2.5mm hook
- Yarn, CGOA Presents: Sparkle #08

Cardigan Sweater

Finished size: Approximately 1¾" high by 3¾" wide. Gauge: 7 sc and 7 rows = 1".

Instructions

1. Cardigan back is worked the same as the Sleeveless Top back.
2. Cardigan fronts are worked the same as the Sleeveless Top front from Rows 1 - 7.
3. Cut yarn, pull end through last loop on hook.
4. Work the sleeves exactly the same as the sleeves for the pullover sweater.

Materials

- 2.5mm hook
- Yarn, CGOA Presents: Splendor #4

Materials

- 2.5mm hook
- Yarn, CGOA Presents: Frolic #07

◀ Skirt

Finished size: Approximately 2¼" high by 2½" wide. Gauge: 7 dc and 3 rows = 1".

Instructions

Begin: Ch 30. Join.
Row 1: Ch 3 (counts as first dc), 1 dc in each remaining ch. (30 dc) Join last dc to top of ch 3.
Rows 2 - 5: Ch 3 (counts as first dc), 1 dc in each remaining dc. (30 dc) Join last dc to top of ch 3.
Row 6: Ch 4, skip 2 dc, * 1 dc, ch 1, skip 2 dc, 1 dc in next dc*. Repeat from * to * to end of round. (10 dc/ch 1 sp). Join last ch to 3rd ch of the beginning ch 4. Cut yarn, weave end into skirt.
Belt: With two strands held together: Ch 30. Cut yarn, pull ends through last loop on hook. Weave in and out of ch 1 spaces, starting and ending at center front.

Vest ▶

Finished size: Approximately 1¼" high by 1¼" wide. Gauge: 7 sc and 7 rows = 1".

Instructions

Ch 14 and work in sc, following graph. Stitch shoulder fronts to shoulder backs.

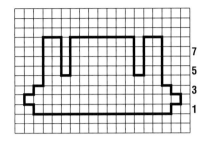

Materials

- 2.5mm hook
- Yarn, CGOA Presents: Frolic #08

Materials

- 2.5mm hook
- Yarn, CGOA Presents:
  Blithe #08 for sleeves and bodice
  Blithe #06 for skirt and collar

◀ Dress

Finished size: Approximately 2¾" high by 3¾" wide. Gauge: 7 dc and 3 rows = 1".

Instructions

Begin: With the sleeves and bodice section, ch 26 in lilac.

Row 1: 1 sc in 2nd ch from hook, and in each ch. (25 sc) ch 1, turn.

Rows 2 - 4: 25 sc, ch 1, turn.

Row 5: 10 sc, ch 5 for opening, skip 5 sc, 1 sc in each remaining sc, ch 1, turn.

Row 6: 10 sc, 1 sc in each of 5 ch, 10 sc, ch 1, turn.

Rows 7 - 10: 25 sc, ch 1 turn. At end of Row 10, cut yarn, leaving 12" for sewing.

Thread the yarn end into a darning needle. On first sleeve, stitch together the edges for 10 sc from the cuff towards the center. Run the needle through the center 5 sc, sew remaining 10 sc of sleeve edge closed. Stitch in place at end of seam to anchor, and weave end inside sleeve to hide it. Trim end.

Skirt:

Row 1: Join plum color at edge of the 5 sc waist opening. Ch 3 (counts as first dc) and 1 dc in same stitch. 2 dc in remaining 4 sc of this side of waist opening, then 2 dc in each of the 5 sc of the second side. Join last dc to top of ch 3 (20 dc).

Row 2: Ch 3, 1 dc in same sp as ch 3, 1 dc in next dc, *2 dc in next dc, 1 dc in next dc*, repeat from * to * 9 times, join last dc to top of ch 3 (30 dc).

Rows 3 - 5: Ch 3, 29 dc join (30 dc).

After last round, cut yarn, pull end through loop on hook, weave end into skirt.

Collar (optional):

Starting at center back of collar with plum, ch 4.

Row 1: 1 sc in 2nd ch from hook, 1 sc in next 2 sc (3 sc) ch 1, turn.

Row 2: 2 sc in first sc, 1 sc in next sc, 2 sc in last sc (5 sc) ch 1, turn.

Row 3: 2 sc in first sc, 1 sc in next 3 sc, 2 sc in last sc (7 sc) ch 1, turn.

Rows 4 - 10 (working one side of collar): 1 sc in 3 sc, ch 1, turn.

Row 11: Skip first sc, 1 sc in each remaining 2 sc, ch 1, turn.
Row 12: Draw up a loop in each of the 2 sc, yo, pull through all loops on hook. Cut yarn, leaving a 3" end for sewing, pull end through last loop. Join yarn to edge of Row 3, ch 1, and work R 4 - 12 for second side of collar. Tie a knot with ends of Row 12. Thread ends into darning needle. Stitch the knot at the collar front to front of dress. Take yarn ends inside dress. Cut another short piece of yarn and use it to sew the center of the neck edge of the collar to the back neck opening of the dress. Weave in all other loose ends.

Poncho ▶

Finished size: Approximately 2¾" high by 2¾" wide. Gauge: 7 sc and 7 rows = 1".

Instructions

Make two rectangles: Ch 21.
Row 1: Work 1 sc in 2nd ch from hook (20 sc).
Rows 2 - 10: 20 sc, ch 1, turn. At end of Row 10, cut yarn, leaving a 6" tail for sewing.
Sew short end of one rectangle to long edge of other.

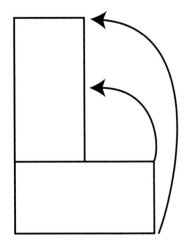

Turn over, and stitch the short side of the other to the long side of the first one.

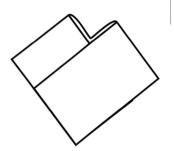

Materials

- 2.5mm hook
- Yarn, CGOA Presents: Blithe #03

Materials

- 2.5mm hook
- Yarn, CGOA Presents: Splendor #03

Shawl ▲

Finished size: Approximately 2" high by 5½" wide (including fringe).
Gauge: 7 sc and 7 rows = 1". *Note: The fringe is chained at the same time as the body of the shawl.*

Instructions

Begin: Ch 37.
Row 1: 1 sc in 13th ch from hook, 1 sc in remaining 24 ch (25 sc). Ch 12 and turn.
Rows 2 - 12: Draw up a loop in each of the first 2 sc, yo, pull through all 3 loops on hook, sc across row to last 2 sc. Draw up a loop in each of the last 2 sc, yo, pull through all 3 loops on hook, ch 12 for the fringe and turn (each row is dec by 2 sc).
Row 13: 1 sc in last sc, cut yarn, pull end through loop on hook; weave in yarn end.

Hat ▶

Finished size: Brim is approximately 1¾" in diameter. Gauge 7 sc and 7 rows = 1".

Instructions

Begin: At center of crown, ch 3, join to form ring.
Row 1: 7 sc in ring, join, ch 1.
Row 2: 2 sc in next 3 sc, 3 sc in next sc, 2 sc in last 3 sc (15 sc) join, ch 1.
Rows 3 - 5: 15 sc, join, ch 1.
Row 6: ch 2 more to form a ch 3, then dc in same space, *3 dc in next sc, 2 dc in next sc*, repeat from * to * to end of round. Join last dc to top of ch 3. Cut yarn, weave in end.

Materials

- 3mm hook
- Yarn, CGOA Presents: Splendor #05

Bag ▶

Finished size: Bag is approximately 1½" high, not including handle. Gauge: 7 sc and 7 rows = 1".

Instructions

Begin: Ch 3, join with a sl st to form ring.
Row 1: 6 sc in ring, join last sc to first with sl st. ch 1.
Row 2: 2 sc in each sc (12 sc). Join, ch 1.
Row 3: *2 sc in first sc, 1 sc in next sc*, Repeat from * to * to end of round (18 sc). Join, ch 1.
Rows 4 - 8: 18 sc, join, ch 1.
Row 9: Working flat for sides of bag: 6 sc, ch 1, turn.
Rows 10 - 4: Skip the first sc, 1 sc in each remaining sc. after Row 14, there will only be 1 sc. Cut yarn, draw through last loop on hook.
Second side: Skip 3 sc, join yarn and repeat R 10 - 14. After Row 14, do not cut yarn.

Materials

- 2½mm hook
- Yarn, CGOA Presents: Splendor #03

Strap ▶

You can work the cord in two ways: Ch 15, join with a sc to the last sc of other side. Ch 1, and work a sl st in each ch. Join with sl st to last sc of the bag side. Cut yarn, pull end through last loop on hook. Weave in ends.

Or: *Ch 2, sl st in 2nd ch from hook*. Repeat from * to * 15 times. Join to top of first side of bag.

Note: This little bag works well as an Amulet Bag.

The Amulet Bag in the photo was made with CGOA Presents Splendor #4 and a 3mm hook. You will need to lengthen the cord so it will go around your neck. You can either ch 150 and sl st in each cord or repeat from * to * 150 times.

When you crochet the Pocket Dolly's Hat and Bag in raffia, they will look like straw and be large enough for a much bigger doll.

▼ Chair

The Pocket Dollies really need a comfy armchair. Gauge: 7 sc and 7 rows = 1".

Instructions

Chair back: Make 1: Ch 6.

Row 1: 1 sc in 2nd ch from hook, and in each remaining ch (5 sc). Ch 1.

Rows 2 - 5: 2 sc in first sc, 1 sc in each sc to last sc, 2 sc in last sc (7 sc in Row 2; 9 sc in Row 3; 11 sc in Row 4; 13 sc in Row 5).

Rows 6 - 40: 13 sc, ch 1, turn.

Rows 41 - 44: Draw up a loop in each of the first 2 sc, yo, pull through all 3 loops on hook, 1 sc in each sc to last 2 sc, draw up a loop in each of the last 2 sc, yo, pull through all 3 loops on hook (11 sc in Row 41; 9 sc in Row 42; 7 sc in Row 43; 5 sc in Row 44).

Cut yarn, leaving a 12" tail for sewing, draw through last loop on hook.

Fold chair back in half, and stitch outer edges shut, leaving an opening for stuffing. Stuff. Sew shut.

Chair Base: Make one: Ch 12.

Row 1: 1 sc in 2nd ch from hook, (11 sc).

Materials

- 2.5mm hook
- Yarn, CGOA Presents:
  Frolic #09 for back, base, sides of arms
  Frolic #06 for seat, ends of arms and feet
- Small amount of polyester stuffing

Rows 2 - 18: 11 sc, ch 1, turn.
Fold chair base in half, and stitch outer edges shut, leaving an opening for stuffing. Stuff. Sew shut.
Chair Seat: Ch 10.
Row 1: 1 sc in 2nd ch from hook, and in each of remaining sc, ch 1, turn (9 sc).
Rows 2 - 18: 9 sc, ch 1, turn.
Fold chair seat in half, and stitch outer edges shut, leaving an opening for stuffing. Stuff. Sew shut.
Arm ends: Make four. Ch 4.
Row 1: 1 sc in 2nd ch from hook, 1 sc in each of last 2 ch (3 sc). Ch 1, turn.
Row 2: 1 sc in each of first 2 sc, 2 sc in last sc, ch 1, turn (4 sc).
Row 3: 4 sc, ch 1, turn.
Row 4: 1 sc in each of first 2 sc, draw up a loop in each of the last 2 sc, yo, pull through all 3 loops on hook; ch 1, turn (3 sc).
Row 5: Draw up a loop in each of the first 2 sc, yo, pull through all 3 loops on hook, 1 sc in last sc, ch 1, turn (2 sc).
Row 6: 2 sc, ch 1, turn.
Row 7: 2 sc in first sc, 1 sc in each of next 2 sc, ch 1, turn (3 sc).
Row 8: 1 sc in first 2 sc, 2 sc in last sc, ch 1, turn (4 sc).
Row 9: 2 sc in first sc, 1 sc in each of next 3 sc, ch 1, turn (5 sc).
Row 10: 5 sc, ch 1, turn.
Row 11: Draw up a look in each of the first 2 sc, yo, pull through all 3 loops on hook, 1 sc in next sc, draw up a loop in each of the last 2 sc, yo, pull through all 3 loops on hook, ch 1. Cut yarn, pull end through last loop, leaving a tail of 9" for stitching. Place a small safety pin along Row 1 to make orientation of arms clear when sewing up the arms.
Arm sides: Make two. Ch 31.
Row 1: 1 sc in 2nd ch from hook, and in each of remaining sc, ch 1, turn (30 sc).
Rows 2 - 30: 30 sc, ch 1, turn.
Sew edges of side of arms to edges of arm ends.
Leave ends of the side piece open for stuffing. Stuff and sew shut.
Feet: Make four. Ch 3, join to form ring.
Row 1: 7 sc in ring, join, ch 1.
Row 2: 2 sc in each sc, join, ch 1 (14 sc).
Rows 3 - 4: 14 sc, join, ch 1.
Row 5: (Draw up a loop in 2 sc, yo, pull through all 3 loops on hook) a total of 7 times (7 sc), join, ch 1. Cut yarn, leaving a 5" end for sewing, pull end through last loop on hook. Stuff.

Assembling Chair

1. Stitch edges of arms to edges of back.
2. Stitch edge of base to folded edge of back and lower edges of arms.
3. Stitch seat to base.
4. Stitch feet to base of chair.

Materials for Small Pouch

- 2mm hook
- Yarn, CGOA Presents:
  Splendor #01 Blue/Violet/Aqua
  Splendor #04 Purple/Rust/Mint
- Pewter button

Materials for Large Pouch

- 3.75mm (F) hook
- 3 spools of Nylon Cord EA131 (96 lb) from
  Lee Valley (Note: This is not fishing line.)
- Pewter button

◀ Pocket Dolly Pouch

After I finished the Pocket Dolly, I thought, "Hmmm ... what if you don't have a pocket to carry her in?" The answer was: "Crochet a pouch to carry her and her clothing!" It also works well for carrying other small treasures. Finished size of small pouch: Approximately 4½" high by 3¾" wide; gauge: 7 sc and 7 rows = 1". Finished size of large pouch: Approximately 8" high by 6½" wide. Gauge: 9 sc and 9 rows = 2".

Instructions

Back: Follow chart from Rows 1 - 66, then ch 12 and join to last sc of R 66 with a sl st. Cut yarn, pull through last loop on hook.
Front: Follow chart from Rows 1 - 38.

Finishing

1. Pin front to back. *Note: When working around a curve, it is sometimes necessary to work at least 2 sc in the same space so the edge won't pull in.*
2. Starting at lower point, and working through both layers of pouch, sc up side of pouch to Row 38, then ch 125 and join to other side at Row 38. Ch 1, 1 sc in each ch back to the start of the chain.
3. Now, continue working sc around outside edge of pouch, up to tip of flap. Work 15 sc in the 12 chain loop at the tip of the flap.
4. Continue working sc from tip of flap down side to lower point. Join last sc to first with sl st, and take ends inside pouch.
5. Sew button to front of pouch

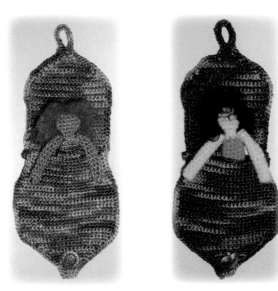

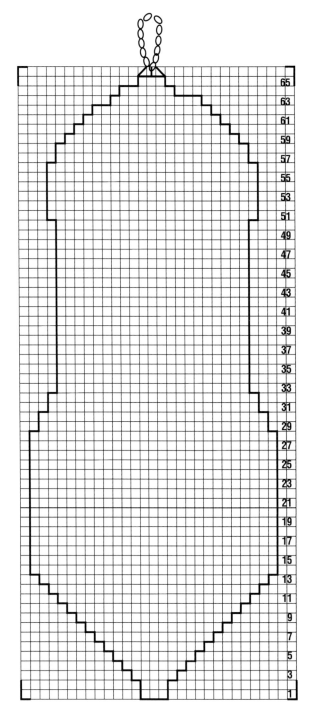

65
63
61
59
57
55
53
51
49
47
45
43
41
39
37
35
33
31
29
27
25
23
21
19
17
15
13
11
9
7
5
3
1

Three Panel Screen Pattern

Center of →
back panel

Cut 2
*front panels
for Triptych Doll*

Cut 1
*on fold for back
of Triptych Doll*

Cut 3
*on fold for
Three Panel Screen*

▲Small Nylon Cord Doll

The large pouch has a Basic Doll appliquéd to the flap.
Finished size: 5". Gauge: 7 sc and 7 rows = 1".

Materials

- 2.5mm hook
- 1 spool of Nylon Cord EA 129 from Lee Valley 45 lb (Note: This is not fishing line)

Instructions

Follow Basic Doll pattern on pages 44 and 45, and stitch or glue to flap of pouch.

Three Panel Screen

When I was making the Pocket Dolly's Pouch, I realized that the shape, with a few modifications, would make a wonderful little screen. It's a very good way of displaying dolls. Just pin them on the screen. Gauge: 7 sc and 8 rows = 2". Finished size of screen: 19" wide by 11" tall.

Instructions

Crocheted screen panels: Make 6.
Row 1: Ch 4. 1 sc in 2nd ch from hook and 1 sc in remaining 2 ch. (3 sc). C 1, turn.
Row 2: 3 sc, ch 1, turn.
Row 3: 2 sc in first sc, 1 sc, 2 sc in last sc, ch 1, turn (5 sc).
Row 4: 2 sc in first sc, 3 sc, 2 sc in last sc, ch 1, turn (7 sc).
Row 5: 2 sc in first sc, 5 sc, 2 sc in last sc, ch 1, turn (9 sc).
Row 6: 2 sc in first sc, 7 sc, 2 sc in last sc, ch 1, turn (11 sc).
Row 7: 2 sc in first sc, 9 sc, 2 sc in last sc, ch 1, turn (13 sc).
Row 8: 2 sc in first sc, 11 sc, 2 sc in last sc, ch 1, turn (15 sc).
Row 9: 2 sc in first sc, 13 sc, 2 sc in last sc, ch 1, turn (17 sc).
Row 10: 2 sc in first sc, 15 sc, 2 sc in last sc, ch 1, turn (19 sc).
Row 11: 2 sc in first sc, 17 sc, 2 sc in last sc, ch 1, turn (21 sc).
Rows 12 - 40: 21 sc, ch 1, turn.
Cut yarn, pull end through last loop on hook.

Materials

- 4.5mm hook
- 4 balls of Lily Sugar 'n Cream Teal
- 3 pieces of corrugated cardboard 8" x 10" each
- Pencil to trace pattern
- Scissors
- Craft knife
- Darning needle

Finishing

1. Trace pattern onto cardboard three times and cut out with sharp craft knife.
2. Lay one crocheted panel on top of another and, working through both layers, work sc around sides and upper edge. You will need to work several sc in the same stitch when you are working around the curves and the point.
3. Slip one of the cardboard sections between the crocheted layers and work sc across the lower edge. Cut yarn, pull end through last loop on hook. Repeat for the other two sections of the screen.
4. Lay the three panels side by side and stitch the edges together.

Triptych Doll ▲

As soon as I had finished the three-panel screen I realized that, with slight modifications, it would make a wonderful doll. Finished height of doll: Approximately 12", not including hair. Gauge: 7 sc and 8 rows = 2".

- 4.5mm hook
- 3.5mm hook
- Yarn, CGOA Presents:
  Splendor #05, Sparkle Gold and Blithe #20, 1 strand of each held together;
  Splendor #03, Sparkle Moonbeams and Graceful #09, 1 strand of each held together;
  Blithe #18, 3 strands held together for face
- Sturdy corrugated cardboard:
  7" x 10" for center section
  3" x 4" for face
  3" x 10" for fronts, 2
- Sturdy paper (business cards or pieces of watercolor paper):
  2" x 3½" each for fronts, and 2 pieces for backs for mask
  3" x 4" for face
- Lightweight cardstock to stabilize mask: 2 pieces, 2" x 3½" each
- Sharp craft knife
- Fabric glue
- Scissors
- Darning needle
- Erasable marker
- Embroidery floss
- 10 red "e" beads
- Needle and nylon thread for sewing on beads
- Pencil crayons
- 2 straight pins
- Blusher and eye shadow or pencil crayons for crocheted face

Instructions

Trace and cut out from cardboard:
    1 face
    2 fronts (half of screen panel)
    1 center panel

Crochet: Three screen panels in the gold color yarn with 4.5mm hook; one screen panel in the Silvery Blue color yarn with 4.5mm hook; one face (follow graph) with skin tone with 3.5mm hook; one back of head (follow graph) with Silvery Blue color yarn with 3.5mm hook; four butterflies with Silvery Blue color yarn (pattern on page 39) with 4.5mm hook; two hands with Silvery Blue color yarn (pattern on page 28) with 3.5mm hook; one heart with Silvery Blue color yarn (pattern on page 26) with 4.5mm hook; two small flowers with Silvery Blue color yarn (pattern on page 38) with 3.5mm hook.

Body center: Lay silver panel on top of gold panel and working through both layers, sc around the sides and the upper edge. When turning corners, you will need to work more than l sc in a single stitch. Slip the cardboard panel inside the crocheted layers, and work sc across the lower edge. Cut yarn, pull end through last loop on hook. Take yarn end inside.

Fronts: Fold one gold panel in half. Starting at top point, and working through both layers, sc down the side. Slip the cardboard panel inside and work sc across lower edge. Cut yarn, pull end through last loop on hook. Take yarn end inside. Stitch or glue hands and butterflies to front panels and butterflies to inside. Stitch front panels to center panels at side edges. Sc around crocheted heart and stitch it to center panel, leaving the top edge open so that it can be used as a pocket to hold treasures. Ch st trim: Ch approximately 32" with Silvery Blue color yarn and glue it to body, in a zigzag pattern.

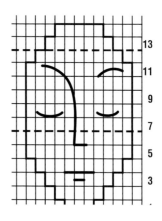

Draw the features of the face with an erasable marker. Embroider the face. Shade it with eye shadow and blusher or pencil crayons. Lay the face on top of the back of the head and, working through both layers, with the Silvery Blue yarn sc from Row 5, around sides across top and down to other end of Row 5. Then, sc across the lower edge only of the face section, then ch 1 and sc across the lower edge only of the Back of Head section. Slip the face onto the point of the center section. Slide the cardboard inside the face so it is against the face, with the point of the center between it and the back of head. Stitch the face and back of head to the center panel.

Hair: Join yarn to the side of the head. *Ch 10, skip 1 sc, sc in next sc*. Repeat from * to * around head. Ch 1, cut yarn, pull end through last loop on hook. Weave in ends. Ch st trim for the face: With Silvery Blue yarn, ch 9, join last ch to first. Ch 39, join last ch to 9th ch from hook. Ch 1, cut yarn, pull end through last loop on hook. Glue around edge of face. Weave in ends.

Heart mask: Trace the pattern, (and cut out the cheek hearts) to make the template. Copy the pattern onto heavy paper twice and cut out. With the darning needle, pierce at each dot. Cut out the cheek hearts with a sharp knife. Enlarge the dot for the eye by inserting point of darning needle and twirling. Stitch a bead at each of the eyebrow dots. Embroider eyelashes, gluing ends of floss to wrong side of mask. Glue photo or painted paper to back of mask, behind cheeks and eyes. Glue mask to lightweight cardboard and cut out. Glue paper to other side of the mask and cut out. Ch st trim: Ch 25 with 4.5mm hook. Glue around outside edge. Glue the mask to the front panels. Glue the two flowers to the top inside of the mask.

Changing the Proportions of the Doll

Remember that the thickness of the yarn you use will determine the finished size of the doll. Thick yarn and a large hook will give you a large doll. A tiny hook and thin thread will give you a small doll.

Shortening the Doll

The Bias Tape/Seam Binding Doll ▼

My mother-in-law had many old packages of seam binding and bias tape that she was not going to use. So, she gave them to me. I thought that it would be really neat to make a doll with them. I figured that the packages had been curled up together for decades in a drawer, and so they should stay together in one project!

When crocheting bias tape, don't use a wooden hook—you risk breaking it. The doll in the photo was made with a size 8mm (L) hook. The finished size of the doll in the photo is approximately 13" from Row 1 to the top of the head (height does not include feet or hair loops). Gauge: 2 sc and 2 rows = 1". She was worked in the round. Because of the size of the stitches when crocheting bias tape, the legs, body, and arms could have fewer rows than the Basic Doll, but the head should still have the same number of rows. The legs have 7 sc and are worked for 11 rounds. The body is worked for 7 rows on 14 sc before the decreases at the shoulders, and the neck and head are worked the same as the Basic Doll pattern. The arms are worked on 6 sc for Rows 1 - 8, then on 3 st for the last round.

I made the face from a 3½" diameter circle of ¼" thick wood. I burned the facial features with a wood-burning tool. I also burned lines around the outside edges of the face. This is optional. The face can also be made with heavy paper that has been glued to cardboard.

Loops of ribbon were glued to the back of the face for hair. Then the face was glued to the head. It's a good idea to weigh the face down with a heavy book after gluing to make sure the glue connects well to the face and head.

Decorative trim was glued around the doll's face. Make hands and feet following directions on pages 31 and 32. Add crocheted flowers, if you'd like (instructions on page 38). It took approximately 25 packages of bias tape to make this doll. One option is to use a bias tape-making tool, and make your own bias tape.

Tall Dolls

Working with thick cord, like jute, makes a tall doll that doesn't need extra rows to give her extra height.

Jute Doll with Wild Green Hair ▶

The Jute Doll, crocheted in the round, with the "in the round" version of the Profile Face is made with jute from Lee Valley. The rounds are not joined but are worked in spirals, in the back bar only of the stitch. This gives the ridged effect. The single crochet in the head is worked normally, under both bars of the single crochet.

Her hands, feet, and the hearts in her hair are made from wood veneer. To attach feet and hands, cut a short length of jute and thread it through the hole. Put a dab of glue into the ankle or wrist and push the ends into the body. She has two black domed buttons ½" in diameter for her eyes and a red button (½" diameter for her mouth). Finished size: 17" not including her hair or her feet. Gauge: 2 sc and 2 rows = 1". Her hair is roving from Fleece Artist.

Instructions

1. Attach the roving in exactly the same way as the ponytails on page 35.
2. Wooden hearts have been glued to the base of the roving tufts.

Heart-Shaped Bag ▶

Instructions

You can make a heart-shaped bag for the Jute doll with an 8mm hook.
1. Crochet two hearts, using the Small Heart chart on page 26. When you work the heart, finish the first bumpy bit at the top of the heart, then sl st across and over and down to start Row 9 of the second bumpy bit. At the end of Row 10 of the second bump, sl st down to the "shoulder" of the heart at Row 8. Lay this heart on top of the first one, and sc through both to attach them to each other.
2. Ch 25, for the handle, then sc through both layers at the other side.
3. Work down the side and around the heart with sc. You'll have to work 2 and 3 sc in the same stitch sometimes, to allow for the curves.
4. Handle: Work 1 sl st in each ch. Then ch 1 and work sc across the top of one of the hearts. Ch 1 and work sc across the top of the other heart.
5. Cut jute (or yarn, if you are making it in yarn), pull end through last loop on hook, and weave end into bag.
(Note: You can also make it in yarn or nylon cord to wear around your neck. Make the chain longer to fit.)

Materials

- 8mm hook
- Yarn: Jute from Lee Valley

chapter four

Creative Variations:

Lovely Ladies,

Button-jointed Dolls,

Geometrics, and Zaftigs

Lengthening the Doll to Change Her Proportions

If you add rows or rounds to the arms and legs, they will make a doll that is taller looking and more elegant. Usually, I add five rows or rounds to each of the arms and legs. I don't lengthen the body, as simply lengthening the arms and legs gives the doll enough additional height.

The Basic Doll on the right, and her Tall Doll sister on the left, with more rows in her arms and legs.

◀ A Tall Doll with a Paper Face

This tall doll was crocheted with chenille from CGOA and a 3.5mm hook. She has a paper face, and fabric strips for her turban, shawl, and skirt. They are pulled through stitches to hold them in place. She's about 10" tall.

▼ Another Roving Doll

The Roving Doll in this photo was made with roving from the Fleece Artist. The doll was crocheted with White Lily Sugar 'n Cream and a 4mm hook. The legs have 20 rounds of 7 sc and the arms have 11 rounds of 6 sc. The body and head are made following the Basic pattern. The flowers on her forehead and the heart on her chest were crocheted with #8 Perle Cotton and a 1.5mm hook. See instructions on pages 38 and 26. Her hands and feet were both crocheted with embroidery floss and a 2.5mm hook. See page 28 for instructions for hands. Each Foot is Noreen's Crocheted Butterfly (see page 39). It is folded in half, stitched around the outside and then stitched to the end of the leg. The hair is mohair bouclé from the Fleece Artist. She is wrapped with the roving. The wings are made by tying yarn around two loops of roving and then stitching it to her back.

▲ Tall Glittery Doll in a Mask

This glittery doll was made with CGOA Presents Razzle #11 and #12 and a strand of CGOA Presents Graceful #06, all held together and crocheted with a 4mm (G) hook. Her hair is held in place with paper beads (see pages 19 and 55). She wears a brass mask from Fancifuls Inc. that was painted with nail polish. Her wings are the Favorite pattern on page 34.

Paper Bead Crown Tall Doll ▶

She is approximately 9½" tall, including her crown. Gauge: 5 sc and 5 rows = 1". There are 20 rounds in each leg and 15 rounds in each arm. The head and body are worked the same as the Basic Doll pattern. A little blusher was rubbed on her cheeks, and a little eye shadow was rubbed on her eyelids.

Instructions to make her crown

1. Glue or stitch crocheted face to the head.

2. Stitch five long tapered paper beads (see instructions on page 19) around the face.

3. Punch dots out of a magazine photo and glue them over the spaces between the beads.

4. Following diagram, stitch long beads around head.

Anchor yarn in head. Take darning needle through 1 long bead, 1 short bead, 1 long bead and into head. Come up through long bead and then through short horizontal bead.*Go through 1 short bead and 1 long bead and into head.Come out through previous long bead, and the short one.* Repeat from * to *.

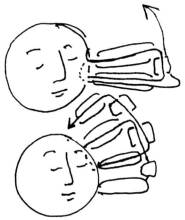

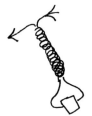

5. To make the each bead for the necklace: Wrap 20-gauge wire around the end of a 5mm crochet hook for an inch. Make five.

6. For the collar: Make a coil that is 3" long and wrap around her neck. Join ends by bending them over each other. Glue a paper dot over joint if necessary.

7. For cuffs around ankles and wrists, make 2" long coils and wrap around each wrist and ankle. Join.

8. To stitch on the five dangling beads, anchor yarn at neck, go through wire coil, pick up short paper bead, go back up through wire coil bead and back into neck. Repeat for other four beads.

9. Glue a paper dot at the end of each short paper bead.

Paper Dots

1. Punch out dots from a photo from a magazine, or from decorative paper. Glue them over any gaps in crown, and down front of doll body, arms, and legs.

2. To glue the dots to the doll, put a dab of glue in a saucer or on a plastic lid, and pick up a little with a toothpick. Smear a little glue onto the back of the dot, and with tweezers, stick it to the doll.

Materials

For body:
- 4mm (G) hook
- Yarn, 1 strand CGOA Presents:
  Grace #09
  Frolic #09
  Kid Mohair #015

For face:
  2mm hook
- Yarn, CGOA Presents:
  Blithe #18 and then embroidered
  (see instructions page 23)

◀ Tall Doll with Many Wings

The dots on this doll were made by punching out watercolor paper that had swirls of acrylic paint on it. The doll in the photo was worked with one strand of each of: 4 sc and 4 rows = 1". She is approximately 9½" tall, not including her hair. There are 20 rounds in each leg and 15 rounds in each arm. The head and body are worked the same as the Basic Doll pattern. The wings are made in single crochet from the Simple Triangular Wings pattern on page 34.

Instructions

1. Crochet four wings.
2. Trace four little hearts for wings and one larger heart for chest onto re-enforced wood veneer. Go over the shapes with wood-burner.
3. Cut out the hearts and glue the large one to the chest of doll.
4. Stitch wings to upper arms of doll and to lower legs.
5. Glue dots around heart on chest and close to edges of wings.
6. Glue the smaller hearts to the wings close to the dots.
7. Glue dots around the wrists and ankles.
8. For the face: Trace the shapes onto re-enforced (with cardboard) wood veneer.
9. Draw the shapes with a wood burner. Cut out the shapes and glue them to face.
10. Glue dots around the face.
11. Hair is made using the ponytail technique on page 35.
12. Glue dots on each of the ponytails.

Materials

- 4mm (G) hook
- Yarn (Hold all together),
  CGOA Presents:
  Blithe #03
  Celebrity #012
  Kid Mohair #09

Thoughts on Tall Dolls' Arms and Legs

The Tall Dolls made me think … How would they look with joints at their shoulders, hips, elbows, and knees? I figured they'd be very "dance-y," which appealed to me enormously. I used the graph for the Profile Face Doll, and buttons were the perfect solution for the joints of the arms and legs. Finished height of doll: 8½" not including hair.

Bracelet Doll ▶

The Bracelet Doll in the photo was made with: Nylon cord (EA129 from Lee Valley) 3.50mm (E) hook, 2 pewter buttons from CGOA Presents, a hook-and-eye or other closure of your choice. Finished height of doll with her arms up: 7". Gauge: 6 sc and 6 rows = 1". The doll in the photo has 20 rows in her legs and 13 in her arms. The legs are crossed and sewn together, and one end of the closure is sewn to one toe. The arms are crossed behind her head, which is stitched to the arm, and the other end of the closure is sewn to the fingertips. One heart button is sewn to her chest and another one is sewn to her hand.

Instructions for Necklace

1. Make two tall dolls with 20 rows for legs.
2. Make arms as a single unit of 30 rows per doll.
3. Sew arms to doll so they are overhead.
4. Cover the small cabone ring (see page 126) and stitch to center of arm section.
5. Cover three of the larger cabone rings for each doll. Cover half of the first ring, and then cover half of the second, and then the entire third ring. Cover the second half of the second and then the first ring.
6. Cross the legs and sew the cabone rings to the feet of the dolls.
7. Sew the closure to the top of the third cabone rings.
8. Crochet two hearts in sc, following the chart on page 26. Lay one heart on top of the other and, holding them together, sc around one side, down to point. You will need to work several sc in the same stitch as you go around curves. At point, ch 5. Sc up the side. Sc across the upper edge of the top heart. Ch 1 and turn hearts over. Sc across the upper edge of the other heart. Ch 1, cut yarn, pull end through last loop on hook. Weave in ends, and glue to inside of hearts.
9. Sew small cabone rings to "shoulders" of the heart.
10. Weave in any loose ends and glue ends to secure them.

The Tall Doll makes a wonderful bracelet! Here she is on and off the wrist.

Materials

- 3mm hook
- Two spools nylon cord EA 129 from Lee Valley (you might want a third spool, just in case your gauge is different)
- Cabone rings:
  2 ½" diameter
  6 ⅝" diameter
- Hook and eye, or other closure
- Scissors
- Fabric glue

◀ Tall Doll Necklace

Finished height of doll with her arms up: 7½".
Gauge: 6 sc and 6 rows = 1".

The Tall Doll also makes an awesome necklace.

Materials

- 3mm hook (for the heart)
- 1.5mm hook (for the faces)
- Yarn, CGOA Presents: Chenille Blithe #18 Linen
- Small amount of stuffing
- Pin backs
- The Blue Doll has hearts made with wood veneer and copper foil glued around her face.
- The Ruby Doll has flowers (see directions on page 38) crocheted with a 1.5mm hook and embroidery floss.
- The Green Doll has hair made by stitching on Oilslick style "e" beads from CGOA Presents.

▲ Crocheted Heart Face Pin Doll

Gauge of 6 sc and 6 rows = 1".

Instructions

1. Crochet two hearts, following graph on page 26. Crochet one face oval or circle, following graph on page 23.
2. Draw the face with erasable marker, and embroider it.
3. Either glue or stitch face to heart.
4. Glue or stitch embellishments around face.
5. Sew the front to the back and stitch around edges. Stuff lightly.
6. Glue or sew a pin to the back.

Button-joint Doll #1 ▶

Instructions

Following the graph for the Basic Doll in Profile on page 47, make two body sections. Work Rows 1 - 10 in Green and Rows 11 - 19 in skin tone.

Lower legs: Make two. Beginning with the foot: Ch 6, 1 sc in 2nd ch from hook and in each remaining ch. (5 sc). Fold the last sc up to the first and join with a sl st. You will now begin working on the lower leg: Ch 4, join to form ring, pushing foot out of the way.

Row 1: Ch 1, 7 sc in ring, join, ch 1.

Rows 2 - 10: 7 sc, join, ch 1. After Row 10: Work joint loop: Ch 3, skip 3 sc, sc in next sc, ch 1 and turn, 5 sc in ch 3, join to the sc that the ch 3 emerged from. Cut yarn and pull end through last loop. Weave end inside leg.

Upper legs: Make two. Repeat Rows 1- 10 of lower leg, without making foot.

Lower arms: Make two. Beginning with the hand: Ch 6, 1 sc in 2nd ch from hook and in each remaining ch. (5 sc). Fold the last sc up to the first and join with a sl st. You will now begin working on the lower arm: Ch 4, join to form ring, pushing hand out of the way.

Row 1: Ch 1, 6 sc in ring, join, ch 1.

Rows 2 - 7: 6 sc, join, ch 1. After Row 7, work joint loop: Ch 3, skip 2 sc, sc in next sc, ch 1 and turn, 5 sc in ch 3, join to the sc that the ch 3 emerged from. Cut yarn and pull end through last loop. Weave end inside arm.

Upper arms: Make two. Repeat Row 1- 7, of lower arm without making hand.

Finishing

1. Stitch the two doll body and head sections together, using green yarn to stitch body seams, and skin tone to stitch neck and head sections.
2. Stuff body and sew lower edge shut.
3. Use the ponytail technique on page 35 to make tufted hair. Start at edge of head and repeat the tufting process until hair is satisfying to you.
4. Sew heart button to her chest.
5. Sew a button to each shoulder and hip of body.
6. Sew a button to elbow and knee of upper arms and upper legs.
7. Upper arms and legs are buttoned to body, and lower arms and legs are buttoned to upper arms and legs.

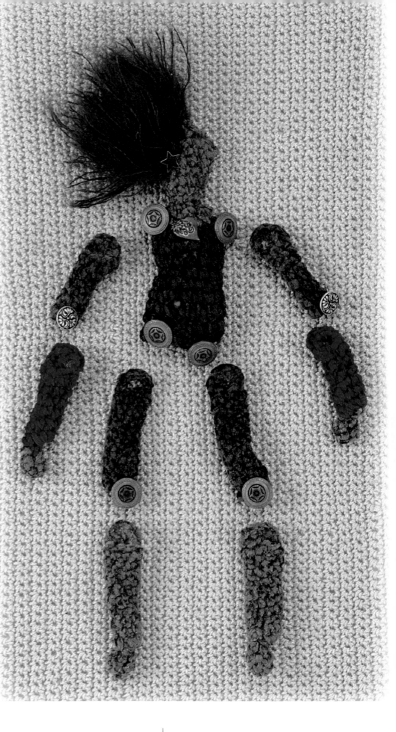

Materials

- 3.25mm (D) hook
- Yarn, CGOA Presents:
  Rayon Chenille #61, 217, 324, 557
  Kid Mohair #16
- 16-gauge wire or a paper clip for earrings
- Needle-nose pliers with a cutting notch to make earrings
- A little stuffing
- Darning needle
- Heart button for chest
- 8 buttons for joints: $1/2$" or $5/8$" diameter

◄ Button-joint Doll #2

And, how about a button-jointed doll using the Basic Doll, straight-ahead head? But that nipped-in waist is appealing, so, here's a shapely Basic Doll with button joints. Finished height of doll: 6½".

Instructions

The Button-joint Doll #2 is worked in the round: Ch 14, join, ch 1.

Row 1: 1 sc in each ch, join, ch 1 (14 sc).
Rows 2 - 4: 14 sc, join, ch 1.
Row 5: * Draw up a loop in each of 2 sc, yarn over hook, draw through all 3 loops on hook *. 1 sc in next 3 sc, repeat from * to * twice, 1 sc in next 3 sc, repeat from * to *, join, ch 1 (10 sc).
Rows 6 - 7: 10 sc, join, ch 1.
Row 8: 2 sc in first sc, 1 sc in next 3 sc, 2 sc in next 2 sc, 1 sc in next 3 sc, 2 sc in last sc, join, ch 1 (14 sc).
Row 9: 14 sc, join, ch 1.
Row 10: Cut body color, join skin tone, 14 sc.
Row 11: Repeat from * to * 7 times, join, ch 1 (7 sc).
Rows 12 - 13: 7 sc, join, ch 1.
Row 14: 2 sc in each sc, join, ch 1 (14 sc).
Rows 15 - 17: 14 sc, join, ch 1. Stuff head now.
Row 18: Repeat from * to * 7 times, join, ch 1 (7 sc).
Row 19: Repeat from * to * 3 times, 1 sc, join, ch 1 (4 sc). Cut yarn, pull end through loop. The arms and legs are made in exactly the same way as Button-jointed Doll #1.

Materials

- 2.5mm hook
- Yarn, CGOA Presents: Frolic #04, 05, 06, 07, 08, 11, 17
- Optional: Brass charm face, hands, and feet from Fancifuls Inc.
- A little stuffing
- Darning needle
- 8 buttons for joints: ½" diameter (the ones I used were a little dull, so, I stuck gold stickers on them)
- If you are using charms, then you'll need fabric glue to attach them to the doll.

Finishing

1. If you are going to use a charm face, then antique it by rubbing black paint on it (optional). Glue to head.
2. If you are using charms for hands and feet, then push them into the wrists and ankles and glue them in place. The crocheted feet act as handy stirrups for holding on the shoe charms.
3. Stuff body and sew lower edge shut.
4. Sew on buttons at shoulders, hips, elbows and knees. Button doll together.

For a different look, try adding charms.

Button-joint Fairy Dolls

As I was working on the button-joint dolls, it occurred to me: Wouldn't these dolls work well with a painted paper head and shoulders? I decided that they would need elegant hands, feet, and wings. The patterns for their heads and shoulders, hands, feet, and wings are on page 97. I think of these as the Button-joint Fairy Dolls. The feathers in the Button-joint Fairy Doll #1's hair were molted by my daughter's budgies. Finished height of doll: 13½" not including hair. Gauge: 4 sc and 4 rows = 1".

Button-joint Fairy Doll #1 ▶

Instructions

1. Make arms and legs just like Button-jointed Doll #1, but do not make crocheted hands or feet.
2. Glue a piece of 6" x 6" card stock to watercolor paper. When dry, cut out, turn over, and glue watercolor paper to the other side. Trace head/shoulders, hands and feet onto the watercolor paper and cut out. Color the paper with washes of ink or paint, if you would like. Draw details on face, hands and shoes. Pierce holes at shoulders.
3. Bend the short piece of wire into a "U" shape. Glue the wire to the back of the doll's head. Glue roving to the doll's head. Then glue feathers around the head like a garland.
4. *Wings:* With permanent marker, trace wing pattern onto plastic. Cut out, and paint with nail polish. Glue wings to back of shoulders.

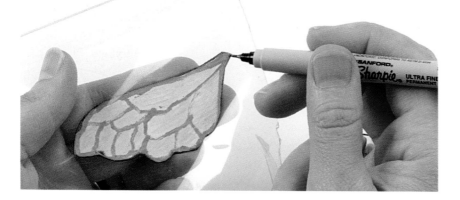

5. *Body:* Work R 1- 10 in Body color, then ch 3 (counts as first dc), and work one round of 14 dc. Join last dc to top of ch 3, ch 1, cut yarn pull end through loop on hook.
6. Stuff body, arms, and legs.
7. Glue the shoulders into the top of the body.
8. Sew the shoulder buttons to the shoulders of the doll. All the other buttons are sewn in the same way as the Button-joint Doll #1.
9. Glue hands inside cuffs, and feet inside legs.

Materials

- 5mm (H) hook
- Yarn, CGOA Presents:
  Ritz Creamy White
  Kid Mohair #01
  Blithe #13
- 3" x 4" sturdy clear reclaimed/ recycled plastic for wings
- Permanent markers and nail polish to color wings
- Lightweight non-corrugated cardboard, such as mat board
- Pencil crayons
- Scissors
- Roving from KDS Fibers for hair
- Feathers
- Stuffing, small amount
- Darning needle
- Heart button for chest (from CGOA Presents)
- 8 buttons for joints, approximately 3/4" diameter (I used vintage ones)
- Scissors
- Short loop of wire for hanging doll (a paper clip is fine)
- Fabric glue

Button-joint Fairy ▶ Doll #2

The other Button-joint Fairy Dolls are made exactly the same as the White one, with minor variations in their hair and wings: The Blue Fairy has buttons from CGOA Presents. Her hair is made by gluing to her head chicken feathers from the craft store, with little bits of roving from KDS Fibers added. Her wings are paper made following instructions on page 93 and the pattern on page 97.

Materials

- Yarn, CGOA Presents:
  Splendor #03
  Kid Mohair #10
  Blithe #22

◀ Button-joint Fairy Doll #3

The Rose Fairy has vintage buttons. Her hair is glued to her head: Torn pieces of painted watercolor paper. Her wings are paper made following instructions on page 93 and the pattern on page 97.

Materials

- Yarn, CGOA Presents:
  Splendor #04
  Kid Mohair #17
  Graceful #07

Materials

- Yarn, CGOA Presents:
  Chenille #217
  Kid Mohair #15
  Graceful 07

▲Button-joint Fairy Doll # 4

The Forest Fairy has vintage buttons. Her hair is glued to her head: Roving from KDS Fibers. Her wings are paper made following Instructions on page 93 and the pattern on page 97. The doll in the photo was made with the listed yarns held together.

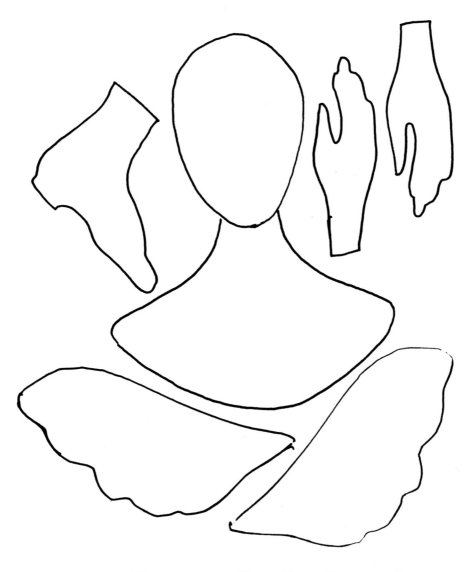

Button-jointed Fairy Dolls Pattern

◄ A Tall Doll with a Beaded Skirt

I really like the mixed-media effect of having the head and shoulders made in paper or wood. I wanted to see how the doll would look with the Basic Doll pattern combined with head and shoulders in paper or wood. The head, shoulders, hands, feet, and heart are all slightly larger than the ones used for the Button-joint Dolls.

Instructions

1. Make head and shoulders, heart, hands and feet (see page 29) from wood veneer or paper. Glue head in place on neck.
2. Work 20 rows for the legs, and then nine rows for the body. Cut cord, pull end through last loop on hook. Work 15 rows of 6 sc for the arms, and do not decrease in last round of arms (see Basic Pattern pages 44 and 45).
3. Glue hands into ends of arms, and feet into ends of legs.
4. Glue shoulders into top of body, then glue heart on chest.
5. Open tops of arms out slightly, then glue to shoulders.
6. Twist skein of yarn into a knot and glue to head.
7. The skirt is made with a single strand of hemp. Thread a tube of "e" beads onto the ball of hemp and push back towards the ball.
   Row 1: Ch 15, join, ch 1. Ch 3, 1 dc in each ch, join (15 sc).
   Row 2: # Ch 3, slide a bead down to ch, ch 3, sc in next dc #.
   Repeat from # to # to end of round, then sc in first ch loop.
   Row 3: * Ch 2, slide a bead down to ch, ch 2, slide a bead down toward last ch,
   ch 2, 1 sc in next ch loop.* Repeat from * to * around skirt (15 ch loops).
   Rows 4 - 6: * Ch 2, slide a bead down to ch, ch 2, slide a   bead down toward last ch,
   ch 2, 1 sc in ch space of next ch loop, between the 2 beads.*
   Repeat from * to * around skirt.
   Row 7: *Ch 7, 1 sc in next chain space*. Repeat around skirt
   Row 8: Ch 3, 1 sc, 1 hdc, 2 dc, ch 4, join to top of last dc, 1 dc, 1 hdc, 1 sc. Repeat from * to * to end of Row (15 shells). Join last ch to first sc, cut cord and weave in end, and glue end into last Row if necessary.
8. Put skirt onto doll, then run a bead of glue around the waist, and around top edge of skirt. Wrap top Row of skirt with a strand of cord. Tie knot and glue end into waistband.

Materials

- 6mm (J) hook
- 2 strands of fine hemp cord (from Heritan) held together (you'll need one ball)
- 1 skein mohair boucle
- 1 tube of "e" beads
- Fabric glue
- Heavy paper (such as old business cards or watercolor paper) or wood veneer glued to lightweight cardstock (I used wood veneer business cards from Lee Valley Tools)
- Pencil crayons or wax crayons
- Wood-burning tool or permanent black felt tip pen
- Carbon paper to trace patterns onto doll parts
- Scissors
- Craft knife

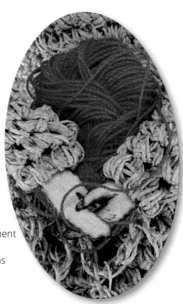

Tall Doll Pattern

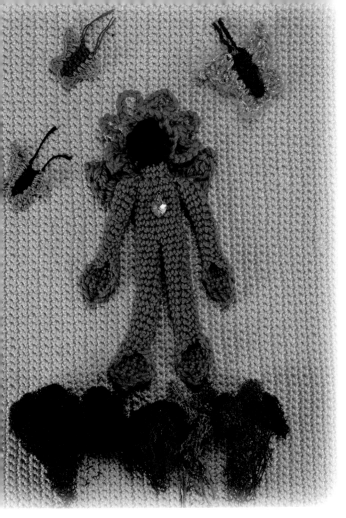

The Flower Tall Doll

The finished Flower Doll is approximately 7" tall. Gauge: 6 sc and 6 rows = 1". She's made taller by adding leaves as hands and feet. The Favorite Wings pattern (on page 34) work nicely as leaves.

Instructions

Make two legs, with green yarn or thread, beginning at tip of toes.

Row 1: Ch 4, 2 dc in 4th ch from hook. Ch 1, turn (3 dc).

Row 2: 2 sc in first dc, 1 sc in next dc, 2 sc in top of turning ch, ch 1, turn (5 sc).

Row 3: 2 sc in first sc, 1 sc in next 3 sc, 2 sc in last sc, ch 1, turn (7 sc).

Rows 4 - 6: 7 sc, ch 1 and turn. At end of Row 6, join last sc to first, ch 1.

Rows 7 - 21: Working in rounds: 7 sc, join, ch 1. At end of first leg, cut yarn, pull end through last loop on hook.

Row 22: On second leg, work 4 sc, then holding first leg so open leaf is at front, work sc around first leg, then complete around second leg. Join, ch 1.

Rows 23 - 30: 14 sc, join, ch 1.

Row 31: *Draw up a loop in each of 2 sc, yo, and pull through all 3 loops on hook *, repeat from * to * 7 times, join, ch 1 (7 sc).

Rows 32 - 33: 7 sc, join, ch 1. Cut Green and join Black yarn.

Row 34: 2 sc in each sc, join, ch 1 (14 sc).

Rows 35 - 38: 14 sc, join, ch 1.

Row 39: Repeat from * to * 7 times, join, ch 1 (7 sc).

Row 40: Repeat from * to * 3 times, skip last sc, join, ch 1 (3 sc). Cut yarn, pull end through last loop on hook.

Blossom: With blossom color, make Wig with Chained Loops on page 36. Sew blossom to head.

Arms: With green, make two, beginning at tip of fingers.

Row 1: Ch 4, 2 dc in 4th ch from hook. Ch 1, turn (3 dc).

Row 2: 2 sc in first dc, 1 sc in next dc, 2 sc in top of turning ch, ch 1, turn (5 sc).

Row 3: 2 sc in first sc, 1 sc in next 4 sc, ch 1, turn (6 sc).

Rows 4 - 6: 6 sc, ch 1 and turn. At end of Row 6, join last sc to first, ch 1.

Rows 7 - 17: 7 sc, join, ch 1.

Row 18: Repeat from * to * 3 times, join ch 1, cut yarn, pull end through last loop on hook.

Sew arms to body and wings to back of body. Optional: Sew heart charm to chest.

Materials

- 2.5mm hook
- Patons Grace, 1 ball each:
  Rose 60437
  Teal 60724
  Night 60040

▲ Celtic Mermaid

The leaves on Tall Flower Doll's Feet looked so much like a mermaid's tail that they inspired me to design the Celtic Mermaid doll. Many years ago I saw a photo of a medieval sculpture of a mermaid; I fell in love with her, and have been working with her ever since. I've made her in cloth, wood, foil, and now, in crochet. I think that this crocheted version is my favorite! Finished height of mermaid: 12". Width from fin-to-fin: 10". Gauge: 4 sc and 4 rows = 1".

𝓜𝓪𝓽𝓮𝓻𝓲𝓪𝓵𝓼

- 4mm (G) hook
- 150 gm Lily Sugar 'n Cream Pale Seafoam (3 balls)
- Darning needle
- Stuffing, small amount
- Fabric glue
- Scissors
- Pins and a piece of cardboard or other surface for pinning
- Cabone ring

Instructions

Make two tails: Starting at tip of tail, 2.

Row 1: Ch 3, 1 sc in 2nd ch from hook, and in last ch. Ch 1, turn (2 sc).

Row 2: 2 sc in each sc, ch 1, turn (4 sc).

Row 3: 2 sc in first sc, 1 sc in next 2 sc, 2 sc in last sc, ch 1, turn (6 sc).

Row 4: 2 sc in first sc, 1 sc in next 4 sc, 2 sc in last sc, ch 1, turn (8 sc).

Row 5: 2 sc in first sc, 1 sc in next 6 sc, 2 sc in last sc, ch 1, turn (10 sc).

Row 6: 2 sc in first sc, 1 sc in next 8 sc, 2 sc in last sc, ch 1, turn (12 sc).

Row 7: 2 sc in first sc, 1 sc in next 10 sc, 2 sc in last sc, ch 1, turn (14 sc).

Rows 8 - 13: 14 sc, ch 1, turn.

Row 14: * Draw up a loop in each of 2 sc, yarn over hook, draw through all 3 loops on hook * 7 times, join, ch 1 (7 sc).

Rows 15 - 17: 7 sc, ch 1, turn.

Row 18: 7 sc, join last sc to first sc, ch 1.

Rows 19 - 100: 7 sc, ch 1.

Building the tail: Copy pattern for tail and place on cardboard or other surface that you can push pins into. Place the tail sections on the pattern, and pin fins in place. Following pattern, form loops and crossovers of the interlaced tail. Pin to hold in place.

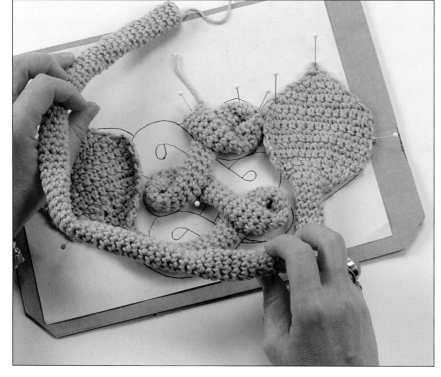

Glue crossing points and places where the tail sections touch each other.

While glue is drying, work on the arms.

Row 1: Make two arms. Ch 4, 2 dc in 4th ch from hook. Ch 1, turn (3 dc).

Row 2: 2 sc in first dc, 1 sc in next dc, 2 sc in top of turning ch, ch 1, turn (5 sc).

Row 3: 2 sc in first sc, 1 sc in next 3 sc, 2 sc in last sc, ch 1, turn (7 sc).

Row 4: Make thumb: (Note: Make 1 thumb at the beginning of Row 4 for one of the arms, and at the end of R 4 for the other arm). The thumb is made by chaining 4, then sl st in 2nd ch from hook and in 2 remaining ch. Continue to work the arm (7 sc).

Rows 5 - 6: 7 sc, ch 1 and turn. At end of Row 6, join last sc to first, ch 1.

Rows 7 - 21: 7 sc, join, ch 1.

Row 22: Repeat from * to * 3 times, skip last sc, join, ch 1. At end of arm, cut yarn, pull end through last loop on hook. Put a dab of glue in the elbow to hold the arm in position.

Body: Place a pin in the last round of the tail to aid in counting rounds.

Row 1: Join yarn to top of tail and work 14 sc, join last to first sc, ch 1.

Rows 2- 9: 14 sc, join, ch 1. Stuff body.

Row 10: *Draw up a loop in each of 2 sc, yo, and pull through all 3 loops on hook *, repeat from * to * 7 times, join, ch 1 (7 sc).

Rows 11 - 12: 7 sc, join, ch 1.

Row 13: 2 sc in each sc, join, ch 1 (14 sc).

Row 14: 14 sc, join, ch 1.

Row 16: 2 sc in first sc, 1 in next sc, repeat from * to * 7 times join, ch 1 (21 sc).

Rows 17 - 18: 21 sc, join, ch 1.

Row 19: *Draw up a loop in each of 2 sc, yo, and pull through all 3 loops on hook *, repeat from * to * 10 times, skip last sc, join, ch 1 (10 sc).

Row 20: Repeat from * to * 5 times, join, ch 1. Stuff head.

Cut yarn, pull end through last loop on hook, then thread into a darning needle and gather last round. Pull up and stitch closed. Take end inside head.

Stitch arms to body.

Make breasts, following pattern for the breasts in the Zaftig Doll on page 122. Stitch them to the body.

Hair

Instructions

Forehead braid: Chain a chain (see page 105) that is 35 large loops. (Ch with a 4mm hook then chain the chain with an 8mm hook.)

Fold 7 chains up at each end and stitch to form the loops.

Hold the braid at the back of the head, and bring the ends around to the front, crossing them over, and placing the loops at the sides of the head.

Coil for top of head: Ch 26. Work 3 sc in 2nd ch from hook and in each ch to end. Sew or glue to top of head.

Braids: Make two. Chain a chain of 15 chained ch.

Twist the living daylights out of it and fold it in half, which will make it twist around itself.

Stitch or glue to the back of the Doll's head.

Cover a cabone ring (see Instructions on page 126) and stitch it to back of head.

The hair is made in four sections: a braid that goes around the forehead and also forms the loops at the side of the head, coils at top of head, and braids that hang down the sides at the back of the head.

How to Make a Chained Chain

To make a chained chain, you simply chain enthusiastically for ages, and don't even bother counting how many. You need lots. You need more. Now, treating your chain as if it were a single strand of yarn and using a hook that is at least two or three sizes larger than your first hook, pull out a long loop in the chain to keep it from unraveling while you are chaining the other end. Beginning at the very first loop, make a loop in the chain and chain your chain. The pattern will tell you how many chained chain loops you will need. When your chained chain is long enough, take either hook through the loop of yarn, then place the last chained chain loop on the hook as well. Pull up on the yarn so it is a normal loop on the hook. YO, and pull through both loops on hook. Cut yarn, yo, and pull end through last loop on hook.

Making Rounder Dolls

Adding stitches to the body gives dolls a charming, chubbier look.

◀The Chubby Doll

Instructions

Rows 1 - 15: Make the arms and legs exactly the same as the Basic Doll pattern. And here is how you'll make a chubby body.

Row 16: Work as normal. Join, ch 1 (14 sc).

Row 17: 2 sc in each sc of previous Row, join, ch 1 (28 sc).

Row 18: 1 sc in each sc, join, ch 1 (28 sc).

Row 19: [2 sc in first sc, 1 sc in next sc] repeat to end of round, join, ch 1 (42 sc).

Rows 20 - 21: 42 sc, join, ch 1.

Row 22: *1 sc, draw up a loop in each of next 2 sc, yo, and pull through all three loops on hook* repeat from * to * to end of round, join, ch 1 (28 sc).

Row 23: 28 sc, join, ch 1.

Row 24: Repeat from * to * to end of round, join ch 1 (14 sc).

Stuff the body with polyester stuffing or your choice of stuffing.

Row 25: Repeat from * to * to end of round, join ch 1 (7 sc).

Rows 26 - 27: 7 sc, join, ch 1.

Row 28: 2 sc in each sc of round, join, ch 1 (14 sc).

Row 29: 2 sc in each sc of round, join, ch 1 (28 sc).

Rows 30 - 31: 28 sc, join, ch 1.

Row 32: Repeat from * to * to end of round, join ch 1 (14 sc).

Stuff the head with polyester stuffing or your choice of stuffing.

Row 33: Repeat from * to * to end of round, join ch 1 (7 sc).

Row 34: 7 sc, join, ch 1.

Cut yarn, thread into darning needle, stitch top of head shut, then take end inside doll.

Fold the feet up and stitch in place.

Chubby Snowman

Instructions

Crochet Snowman: Follow Chubby Doll pattern
(page 106).

Pointy hat:

Row 1: With 3.75mm hook, ch 3, join, ch 1. 5 sc in ring, join, ch 1.

Rows 2 - 3: 5 sc, join ch 1.

Row 4: 2 sc in each sc, join, ch 1 (10 sc).

Row 5: 10 sc, join ch 1.

Row 6: 2 sc in each sc, join, ch 1 (20 sc).

Row 7: 20 sc, join ch 1.

Row 8: *2 sc in first sc, 1 sc in next* repeat to end of round, join, ch 1 (30 sc).

Rows 9 - 10: 30 sc, join, ch 1.

Row 11: 1 sl st in each sc, join, ch 1, cut yarn, pull end through last loop. Weave end into hat.

Scarf: With 3.75mm hook ch 51.

Row 1: 1 sc in second ch from hook, and in each ch to end (50 sc). Ch 1, turn.

Rows 2 - 3: 50 sc, ch 1, turn.

Cut yarn, draw through last loop on hook, and weave ends into scarf.

Finishing

1. Sew the arms to the body.
2. Turn up the feet and stitch to secure.
3. Sew the nose button to the center of the face.
4. Sew two black "e" beads to the face for eyes.
5. Sew 7 black "e" beads in a line for the smile.
6. Sew 2 red "e" beads on for cheeks.
7. Sew heart button to chest.

Materials

- 3.5mm (E) hook
- Yarn (1 strand), CGOA Presents: Ritz White Mohair #01 White
- 9 black "e" beads for eyes and mouth
- 2 red "e" beads for cheeks
- ½" red dome button
- Heart button for chest
- Stuffing, small amount
- Darning needle

For the hat and scarf:
- 3.75mm (F) hook
- Yarn, CGOA Presents: Rhapsody Peacock Splash

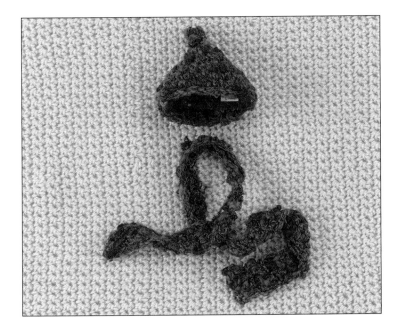

Chubby Teddy Bear ▶

Finished height of
Teddy Bear: Approximately 4½".
Gauge: 6 sc and 6 rows = 1".

Instructions

1. Make Chubby Teddy Bear following Chubby Doll pattern on page 106.
2. At top of head, do not cut yarn.
3. To make ear: Work 5 dc in second round from hook (close up of back of head with arrow pointing to the st). Then, attach ear to head by working 1 sc 2 rounds down. Cut yarn, pull through last loop on hook, then take yarn end inside head.
4. Rejoin yarn at top of head and work second ear in the same way as the first.

Muzzle:
Row 1: Ch 3, join to form ring, ch 1, and then work 7 sc in the ring, join, ch 1.
Row 2: 2 sc in each sc of previous round, join, ch 1 (14 sc).
Rows 3 - 4: 14 sc, join, ch 1. Cut yarn, pull end through last loop on hook.
5. Stuff muzzle and sew to face.
6. Embroider nose and mouth, following diagram on page 59.

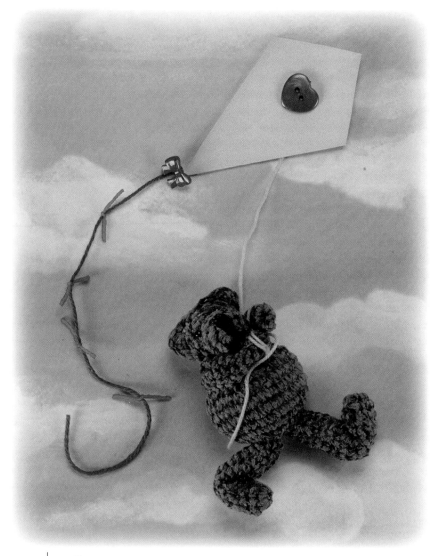

Materials

- 2.5mm hook
- Yarn, CGOA Presents: Chenille #61
- 2 black "e" beads for eyes
- Black embroidery floss or yarn to embroider nose and mouth
- Small amount of stuffing

Bumble Bee Materials

- 2mm hook
- Yarn(1 strand), CGOA Presents:
  Blithe #14 White
  Blithe #02 Black
  Frolic #17 Gold
- Red paper clip for glasses
- Needle-nose pliers to make glasses
- Stuffing, small amount

Chubby Bumble Bee ▶

The Snowman and Teddy Bear are as cute as bugs ... so let's make some bugs!

Instructions

Make Bumble Bee: Follow the Chubby Doll pattern.
Row 1 - 17 in Black.
Rows 18 - 19 in Gold.
Rows 20 - 21 in Black.
Rows 22 - 23 in Gold.
Rows 24 - 25 in Black.
Rows 26 - 27 in Gold.
Rows 28 - 33 in Black.

To make wings: With white and 2mm hook, Ch 5, join to form ring. Ch 4, (counts as first tr), 4 tr in ring (5 tr), turn. Ch 3, (counts as first dc), 1 dc in same st, 2 dc in each tr (10 dc) turn. Ch 2, (counts as first hdc), *yo, draw up a loop in next 2 dc, yo and draw through all loops on hook* repeat from * to * 4 more times (5 hdc), turn. Ch 1, draw up a loop in first 2 hdc, yo, draw through all loops on hook, 1 sc in next hdc, draw up a loop in last 2 hdc, yo, draw through all loops on hook. Ch 1, then sl st in side of edge hdc of Row 3, ch 3, sl st in top of ch 4 of Row 1, ch 4, sc in starting ring. Repeat R 1 - 4 for second wing. Cut yarn weave in end.

Finishing

1. Make pointy hat in black, using a 2mm hook.
2. Sew wings and arms to body.
3. Stitch feet in place.
4. Antennae: Cut a 3"-long piece of black yarn and thread through darning needle. Take end through top of hat and tie a knot.
5. With a red paper clip, make glasses (see instructions page 18). Push arms of glasses into face, and squeeze ends to keep them in place. Glue or stitch if necessary.

Lady Bug Materials

- 2mm hook
- Yarn (1 strand), CGOA Presents:
  Blithe #03 Red
  Blithe #02 Black
- Yellow paper clip for glasses
- Needle-nose pliers to make glasses
- A little stuffing
- Darning needle

Chubby Lady Bug ▶

Instructions

Make the Lady Bug: Follow the Chubby Doll pattern.
Rows 1 - 15 in Black.
Rows 16 - 25 in Red.
Rows 26 - 33 in Black.
Make pointy hat in Black, using a 2mm hook.

Finishing

1. Sew arms to body.
2. Stitch feet in place.
3. With a yellow paper clip, make glasses (see instructions page 18). Push arms of glasses into face, and squeeze ends to keep them in place. Glue or stitch if necessary.
4. Embroider little dots on body.

Butterfly Dolls

If you are going to have a Bumble Bee and a Lady Bug, there must be Butterflies ... right? The patterns for the wings and for the paper face for these Butterflies can be found on pages 31 and 32. The wings were made in paper, wood veneer, and copper. They all have pin backs attached to them so they can be worn as pin dolls. Finished height of black and blue butterflies: Approximately 2½"; gauge: 9 sc and 9 rows = 1". Finished height of the glittery blue butterfly: Approximately 2½"; gauge: 7 sc and 7 rows = 1". The tiny white butterfly bodies were crocheted with #50 crochet cotton that I bought at a garage sale. When it's crocheted with a .5mm hook, the Butterfly body is approximately 1⅛" tall. When a .75mm hook is used, the body is approximately 1⅜" tall. Their wings are made by crocheting CGOA Presents Splendor with a 2.5mm hook and the patterns for Noreen's Favorite Wings and Noreen's Little Butterfly; see pages 34 and 39 for patterns.

Materials for the black Butterflies

- 1.75mm hook
- Yarn, CGOA Presents: Blythe Black

Materials for the dark blue Butterflies

- 1.75mm hook
- Yarn, CGOA Presents: Celebrity #17 Dark Teal

Materials for the glittery blue Butterfly

- 2mm hook
- Yarn, CGOA Presents: Sparkle #08 Moonbeams

Instructions

Butterfly body:
Row 1: Ch 3, join, ch 1. Work 7 sc in ring, join, ch 1.
Rows 2 - 8: 2 sc in first sc, 1 sc in each remaining sc of row, join, ch 1. (Row 2 = 8sc, Row 3 = 9 sc, Row 4 = 10 sc, Row 5 = 11sc, Row 6 = 12 sc, Row 7 = 13 sc, Row 8: 14 sc.)
Row 9: 14 sc, join, ch 1.
Row 10: *Draw up a loop in 2 sc, yo, pull yarn through all 3 loops on hook* Repeat from * to * 7 times, join, ch 1 (7 sc).
Rows 11 - 12: 7 sc, join, ch 1.
Row 13: 2 sc in each sc, join, ch 1 (14 sc).
Rows 14 - 16: 14 sc, join, ch 1.
Row 17: Repeat from * to * 7 times, join, ch 1 (7 sc).
Row 18: Repeat from * to * 3 times, 1 sc in last sc join ch 1 (4 sc). Cut yarn, pull end through last loop on hook.

Finishing

1. Glue the body to the wings.
2. Glue or stitch the pin back to the back of the Little Butterfly, or cover a cabone ring (see instructions page 125) and glue or stitch it to her back.

◀Bunting Bag Baby Doll

If you add a face and hands to the body of the Butterfly, you'll have a baby in a bunting bag! Finished height of doll: Approximately 2½". Gauge: 8 sc and 8 rows = 1".

Instructions

Make doll following Butterfly instructions. If you wish, you can cut 11 lengths of yarn that are 2 feet long each, and tie them together to make a striped doll.

Face: Make with skin tone.

Row 1: Ch 4, 1 sc in 2nd ch from hook and in next 2 ch, ch 1, turn (3 sc).

Row 2: 2 sc in first sc, 1 sc in next sc, 2 sc in last sc, ch 1, turn (5 sc).

Row 3: 5 sc, ch 1, turn.

Row 4: *Draw up a loop in 2 sc, yo, pull yarn through all 3 loops on hook*, 1 sc in next sc; repeat from * to * once, ch 1. Cut yarn, leaving a 6" tail for sewing. Pull end through last loop. Turn the face section so the rows run vertically and sew to head.

Make two hands: With skin tone (or your choice of colors).

Row 1: Ch 3, 1 sc in 2nd ch from hook and in last ch. (2 sc) ch 1, turn.

Rows 2 - 3: 2 sc, ch 1. Cut yarn, leaving a couple of inches for sewing. Tie starting and ending yarns together then thread them into a darning needle and take inside the body.

Optional: Sew or glue a pin back to the back of the doll.

Materials

- 2.5mm hook
- Yarn, CGOA Presents: Frolic #04, 05, 06, 07, 09, 11, 17
- Cherub Charm from Fancifuls, Inc.
- Darning needle

The Shapes that Form the Dolls

When you look at the Basic Doll—especially when she's worked in the flat, you see that the doll is, in a sense, built up out of rectangles. Well, then, why not exaggerate the rectangular aspects of the doll? If her legs are worked as one piece and not divided, it will look like she is wearing a long skirt. This emphasizes her "rectangularity" and is the perfect opportunity to play with tapestry crochet.

Tapestry Crochet

To change colors, work the first half of the sc in the color that you are just finishing up.

Then take the new color over the hook and through to complete the sc.

Carry the yarn from the unused color across the row, and crochet over it.

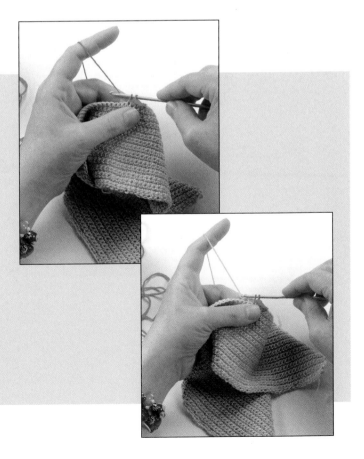

◀ The Long Skirt Doll

Finished height of doll: 4½" tall, not including hair.

Gauge: 7 sc and 7 rows = 1".

Instructions

Feet: Make two.

Row 1: With red yarn, ch 4, join, ch 1. Work 7 sc in ring, join, ch 1.

Rows 2 - 5: 7 sc, join, ch 1. At end of Row 5, cut yarn pull yarn through last loop on hook.

Dress:

R 1: Following chart, join purple yarn and work first 7 sc of Row 1 on one foot, and then the last 7 sc of Row 1 along the second foot. Join, ch 1, join teal yarn.

Rows 2 - 18: Follow chart.

Row 19: With red yarn, *draw up a loop in each of the next 2 sc, yo, pull yarn through all 3 sc on hook*; repeat from * to * 7 times. Join, ch 1. cut blue yarn, join skin tone (7 sc).

Rows 20 - 22: 7 sc, join, ch 1.

Row 23: 2 sc in each sc in row, join, ch 1 (14 sc).

Rows 24 - 25: 14 sc, join, ch 1.

Row 26: *Draw up a loop in each of the next 2 sc, yo, pull yarn through all 3 sc on hook*. Repeat from * to * 7 times. Join, ch 1 (7 sc).

Row 27: *Draw up a loop in each of the next 2 sc, yo, pull yarn through all 3 sc on hook* two times. Draw up a loop in each of the next 3 sc, yo, pull yarn through all 4 sc on hook once. Join. Ch 1, cut yarn, pull through last loop on hook.

Arm: Make one.

Row 1: With purple, ch 4, join, ch 1. Work 6 sc in ring, join, ch 1.

Row 2: 6 sc with purple, join, ch 1.

Rows 3 - 4: 6 sc with teal, join, ch 1.

Rows 5 - 6: 6 sc with red, join, ch 1.

Rows 7 - 8: 6 sc with yellow, join, ch 1.

Rows 9 - 10: 6 sc with purple, join, ch 1.

Rows 11 - 14: 6 sc with skin tone, join, ch 1.

Rows 15 - 16: 6 sc with purple, join, ch 1.

Rows 17 - 18: 6 sc with yellow, join, ch 1.

Rows 19 - 20: 6 sc with red, join, ch 1.

Rows 21 - 22: 6 sc with teal, join, ch 1.

Rows 23 - 24: 6 sc with purple, join, ch 1, cut yarn, pull through last loop on hook.

Wig: Use 2 strands of yellow (or hair color of your choice) and one strand of sewing thread (see instructions for chained loop wig on page 36).

Finishing

1. Sew arms to shoulders.

2. Sew or glue wig to head.

Materials

- 2.5mm hook for doll
- 3.5mm hook for wig
- Yarn, CGOA Presents: Frolic #4, 06, 07, 08, 17
- 2 spools variegated sewing machine thread, (use 1 with each of the 2 working colors held together with yarns used for shoes and dress)
- 1 spool peach color sewing machine thread (hold together with the white yarn for the face and hands)
- Darning needle
- Scissors

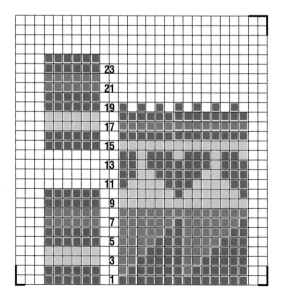

▼ Healing Doll

After I designed and made the Long Dress Doll, I had a wonderful dream that I was teaching a workshop on how to make her. But, the workshop was on making Healing Dolls. The dolls in the dream began as the Long Dress Doll, but soon evolved into amulet bags. Needless to say, I just had to follow this dream! And, so here is the Healing Doll. She can carry anything : a treasured poem, a souvenir rock from a special hike, or even your eyeglasses.

Materials for natural color doll

- 3mm hook
- Nylon cord EA129 from Lee Valley (for all parts of doll except body and cord)
- Body and cord:
- 5mm hook
- Nylon cord EA131 from Lee Valley

Materials for doll with black dress

- 3.5mm hook
- Body and cord:
- Yarn (2 strands), CGOA Presents: Blithe #02
- The rest of the doll:
  2.5mm hook
- Arms: (1 strand) CGOA Presents: Blithe #02
- Skin tone: (1 strand) CGOA Presents: Blithe #20
- Shoes: (1 strand) CGOA Presents: Blithe #03
- Edge of collar, heart, butterfly and flower: (1 strand) CGOA Presents: Splendor #04
- Body of Butterfly and Leaves: (1 strand) CGOA Presents: Blithe #23
- Hair: (2 strands held together) CGOA Presents: Kid Mohair #17
- Darning needle
- Scissors
- A small amount of stuffing for head

Instructions

Feet: Make two feet. With smaller hook and single strand: Ch 3, join, ch 1.

Row 1: 7 sc in Row, join, ch 1.

Rows 2 - 5: 7 sc, join, ch 1.

Body: Use larger hook and thicker cord or two strands of yarn.

Row 1: Work 4 sc of one foot, ch 7, work last 3 sc of this foot, and then work 3 sc of other foot, ch 7, 4 sc of this foot, join, ch 1 (28 st).

Row 2: 4 sc, 1 sc in each of 7 ch, 6 sc, 1 sc in each of 7 ch, 4 sc, join, ch 1 (28 sc).

Rows 3 - 7: 28 sc, join, ch 1.

Rows 8 - 17: *Pull up a loop in each of first 2 sc, yo, pull through all 3 loops on hook*, 1 sc in each sc to end of row, join, ch 1 (18 sc at end of R 17).

Rows 18 - 21: 18 sc, join, ch 1.

Row 22: To begin collar, you will need to sneak over to the edge stitch. You do this by sl st in the back bar of 5 sc. Ch 2 and turn. 1 sc in 2nd ch from hook and in 9 sc, ch 2 and turn.

Row 23: 1 sc in 2nd ch from hook and in 10 sc, ch 1 and turn (11 sc).

Row 24: 11 sc, ch 1 and turn.

Row 25: Repeat from * to *, sc in next 7 sc, repeat from * to *, ch 1, turn (9 sc).

Row 26: 9 sc, ch 1, turn.

Row 27: Repeat from * to *, sc in next 5 sc, repeat from * to *, ch 1, turn (7 sc).

Row 28: 7 sc, ch 1, turn.

Row 29: Repeat from * to *, sc in next 3 sc, repeat from * to *, ch 1, turn (5 sc).

Row 30: 5 sc, ch 1, turn.

Row 31: Repeat from * to *, sc in next sc, repeat from * to *, ch 1, turn (3 sc).

Row 32: 3 sc, ch 1, turn.

Row 33: Pull up a loop in each of 3 sc, yo, pull through all 4 loops on hook, ch 1, cut yarn, pull end through last loop on hook.

Cord: Join to corner of upper edge Ch 100, join to other corner, ch 1. Work a sl st in each ch. Join with a sl st to starting point, cut yarn, tie a knot with the ends and weave ends into inside of dress.

Head: Use lighter cord or one strand of yarn, and make a Profile style head. Stitch to body. (Note: The head of the doll made with yarn needs a little stuffing, but the doll made with cord is sturdy enough to not need stuffing.)

Chained loop wig: Follow Instructions on page 36, and stitch to head.

Arms: Use lighter weight cord (or one strand of yarn) and smaller hook: Ch 5, join, ch 1.

Rows 1 - 33: 6 sc, join, ch 1. (For colored dress: Work 14 Rows dress color, 1 Row trim color, 3 Rows skin tone, 1 Row trim color, 14 Rows dress color.)

Cut yarn, pull end through last loop on hook. Sew arms to shoulders.

Finishing

1. Sc around edge of collar, working 3 sc at point of collar.
2. Crochet a heart, following graph #1 on page 26. Stitch heart to collar.
3. Crochet a flower and a butterfly, following Instructions on pages 38 and 39, and stitch to dress.
4. Stitch lower edges of dress closed.

More Geometry: Triangle and Zaftig Dolls

I have always loved geometry (but not algebra!). For the last few years, I have been intrigued by reading about "Sacred Geometry." Amazing stuff. So, in celebration of geometry, here are some triangle dolls!

Instructions

Legs: Make two, beginning at the foot. Ch 5, join last ch to first chain to form foot. Hold foot out of the way and ch 4. Join to form ring.

Row 1: 4 sc in ring, join, ch 1.

Rows 2 - 15: 2 sc in first sc, 1 in each remaining sc, join, ch 1. At end of Row 15, cut yarn, pull end through last loop on hook.

Body: Adjust legs so the feet are in a pleasing position and then lay them together.

Row 1: Beginning on the right hand side: Call this leg, leg #1. Count 3 sc over from center and join yarn to leg #1. Work 3 sc on front of leg #1, then 3 sc on front of leg #2. Skip 10 sc, then work 4 sc on back, skipping last sc of leg #2. Work 4 sc on back of leg #1, then join last sc to first, ch 1 (14 sc).

Rows 2 - 9: 14 sc, join, ch 1.

Row 10: For the neck, (draw up a loop in next 2 sc, yo, and pull through all 3 loops on hook) 7 times, join, ch 1 (7 sc).

Rows 11 - 12: 7 sc, join, ch 1.

Rows 13 - 20: Increasing to make head, 2 sc in first sc, 1 sc in remaining sc of row. Join, ch 1. (End with 14 sc in Row 20.) At end of Row 20, cut yarn, pull end through loop. Weave end inside.

Make two arms: Work hands in same way as feet.

Work Rows 1 - 14 in the same way as legs.

At end of Row 14, cut yarn, pull end through loop. Use yarn end to sew arm to shoulder. Weave end inside.

Add face, hair, heart, hands and feet of your choice.

Purple Triangle Doll ▶

The Purple Triangle Doll in the photo was crocheted with strips of fabric that were cut about ¼" wide and crocheted with a 5mm (H) hook. The gauge is about 4 sc and 4 rows = 1". She's about 10" tall, not including her hair. She has a strand of beads wrapped around her neck. She has brass charm hands and shoes from Fancifuls Inc. Her heart is crocheted (see graph on page 26) and appliquéd to Favorite Crocheted Wings (see instructions page 34). Her face is crocheted and then embroidered. Face gauge: 10 sc and 10 rows = 1" (see graph on page 23).

Instructions

1. After face is embroidered, rub a little blusher on cheeks and eye shadow on eyes.
2. To make her hair, join yarn to head. Ch 10, cut yarn, pull end through last loop on hook. Repeat as many times as desired.

Materials

- 2mm hook
- Heart: CGOA Presents: Splendor #4
- Wings: CGOA Presents: Splendor # 1
- Face: CGOA Presents: Blithe #18
- Blusher
- Eye shadow

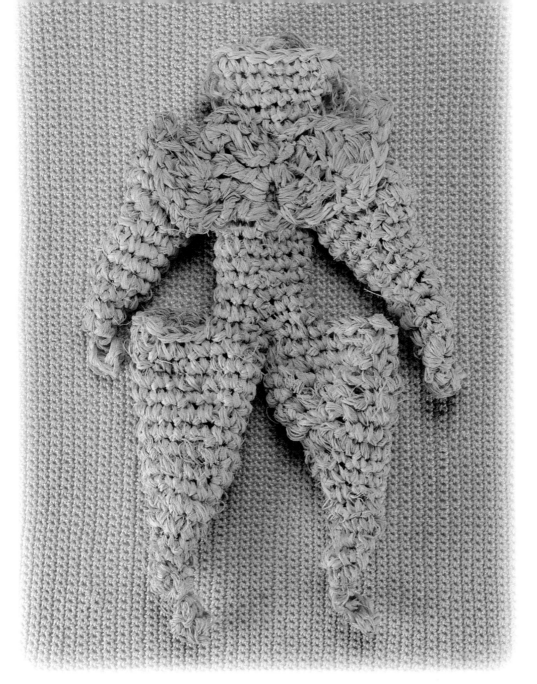

◀Raffia Triangle Doll

The Raffia Doll in the photo was crocheted with strips of raffia from the craft or gardening shop. Pull out a couple of strands from the bundle to make yarn about ¼" wide, and crochet with a 7mm hook. The raffia is in lengths that are about a yard long, so you will have to join them as you crochet. It took one bundle to make the doll, hat, bag, and wings. Do not work with a wooden hook, as the raffia may stress it. She's about 14" tall, not including her hair. The gauge is about 5 sc and 5 rows = 2". She has brass charm hands and shoes from Fancifuls Inc.

◀ Orange Handspun Triangle Doll

The Orange Triangle Doll was crocheted with yarn that I handspun from roving from Fleece Artist. Her hair is unspun roving. Her face is a carved avocado pit. Her heart, teapot, magic wand, and shoes are charms from Fanciful Inc. Her wings are wooden. See page 31 for pattern. She is about 8" tall, from the tip of her toes to the top of her head, not including her hair. See page 24 for instructions on how to carve an avocado pit face.

Instructions

Legs: Beginning at the foot, make two.
Ch 5, join last ch to first chain to form foot. Hold foot out of the way and ch 4. Join to form ring.
Row 1: 4 sc in ring, join, ch 1
Rows 2 - 15: 2 sc in first sc, 1 in each remaining sc, join, ch 1. At end of Row 15, cut yarn, pull end through last loop on hook.
Body: Adjust legs so the feet are in a pleasing position and then lay them together.
Row 1: Beginning on the right hand side, call this leg #1. Count 3 sc over from center and join yarn to leg #1. Work 3 sc on front of leg #1, then 3 sc on front of leg #2. Skip 10 sc, then work 4 sc on back, skipping last sc of leg #2. Work 4 sc on back of leg #1, then join last sc to first, ch 1 (14 sc).
Rows 2 - 9: 14 sc, join, ch 1
Neck:
Row 10: Draw up a loop in next 2 sc, yo, and pull through all 3 loops on hook) 7 times, join, ch 1 (7 sc).
Rows 11 - 12: 7 sc, join, ch 1
Head:
Rows 13 - 20: Increasing to make head, 2 sc in first sc, 1 sc in remaining sc of row. Join, ch 1. (End with 14 sc in R 20.) At end of R 20, cut yarn, pull end through loop. Weave end inside.
Arms: Make 2.
Work hands in same way as feet. Work R 1 - 14 in the same way as legs.
At end of R 14, cut yarn, pull end through loop. Use yarn end to sew arm to shoulder. Weave end inside.
Add face, hair, heart, hands, and feet of your choice.

Zaftig Dolls

The Triangular Dolls are quite "zaftig," which means luscious, curvy, and voluptuous. By just softening the edges of the triangles a little, you end up with a very curvaceous lady. If you want her to be really full-figured, there are optional breasts.

The Teal Zaftig Doll has a Profile Face. Her hair is made from

Materials for Teal Zaftig Doll

- 3.75mm (F) hook
- Yarn (1 strand each held together), CGOA Presents: Rhapsody Peacock Splash Frolic #06
- Beads:
  11 teal wooden ⅜" diameter beads
  9 long tapered paper beads
  9 short straight paper beads
- Pewter heart button from CGOA Presents
- Darning needle

Materials for the Rose Zaftig Doll

- 3.75mm (F) hook
- Yarn (2 strands held together), CGOA Presents: Rhapsody #01
- Crocheted and embroidered face (see page xxx for graph)
- Pewter heart button from CGOA Presents
- Darning needle
- Small amount of stuffing

long tapered paper beads that have a short straight paper bead at the end of each long bead. Her garland is a string of ⅜" diameter teal colored wooden beads from CGOA Presents. (Feel free to use your choice of beads.) Her pewter button is from CGOA Presents. She's not stuffed. She has appliquéd breasts. Finished size of doll: 8½" tall. Gauge: 5 sc and 5 rows = 1".

The Rose Zaftig Doll has the Basic Head with a crocheted face (crocheted in CGOA Presents Blithe #18 with a 2mm hook, then embroidered). Her hat is a brass buckle. Her heart is a brass button. Both are from CGOA Presents. She is stuffed. She doesn't have the bonus breasts. Her hair is a halo of chained loops. Finished size of doll: 10" tall including hair.
Gauge: 4 sc and 4 rows = 1".

Instructions

Make two legs, beginning at foot: Ch 6, work 1 sc in 2nd ch from hook and 1 sc in each remaining ch (5 sc).
Fold and join ends by working a sl st in the end of the first sc.
Tie a knot with the tail of starting yarn to the working yarn coming off the ball.
Leg: Ch 4, join in the sl st on the top of the foot.
Row 1: 7 sc in ring, join, ch 1.
Row 2: 7 sc, join, ch 1.
Rows 3 - 9: 2 sc in first sc, 1 sc in each remaining sc, join, ch 1 (ending with 14 sc in Row 9).
Rows 10 - 15: 14 sc join, ch 1. Cut yarn, pull end through last loop on hook.
Use the tail end of the starting yarn to secure the foot in a pleasing position with a stitch or two.
Row 16: Lay the two legs so the feet are pointing forward. Join yarn at hip and work across 7 sc of one leg, then around the 14 sc of the other leg, and last 7 sc in first leg. Join, ch 1 (28 sc).
Row 17: *Draw up a loop in 2 sc, yo, pull through all 3 sc on hook*; 1 sc in each of next 10 sc, repeat from * to * twice, 1 sc in each of next 10 sc, repeat from * to * once, join, ch 1 (24 sc).
Row 18: *Draw up a loop in 2 sc, yo, pull through all 3 sc on hook*; 1 sc in each of next 8 sc, repeat from * to * twice, 1 sc in each of next 8 sc, repeat from * to * once, join, ch 1 (20 sc).
Row 19: *Draw up a loop in 2 sc, yo, pull through all 3 sc on hook*; 1 sc in each of next 6 sc, repeat from * to * twice, 1 sc in each of next 6 sc, repeat from * to * once, join, ch 1 (16 sc).
Row 20: *Draw up a loop in 2 sc, yo, pull through all 3 sc on hook*; 1 sc in each of next 4 sc, repeat from * to * twice, 1 sc in each of next 4 sc, repeat from * to * once, join, ch 1 (12 sc).
Row 21: 12 sc, join, ch 1.
Row 22: 2 sc in first sc; 1 sc in next 4 sc, 2 sc in each of next 2 sc, 1 sc in next 4 sc, 2 sc in last sc, join, ch 1 (16 sc).
Row 23: 2 sc in first sc; 1 sc in next 6 sc, 2 sc in each of next 2 sc, 1 sc in next 6 sc, 2 sc in last sc, join, ch 1 (20 sc).
Row 24: 2 sc in first sc; 1 sc in next 8 sc, 2 sc in each of next 2 sc, 1 sc in next 8 sc, 2 sc in last sc, join, ch 1 (24 sc).
Row 25: 2 sc in first sc; 1 sc in next 4 sc, 2 sc in each of next 2 sc, 1 sc in next 4 sc, 2 sc in last sc, join, ch 1 (28 sc).
Row 26: 28 sc, join, ch 1.
Row 27: *Draw up a loop in 2 sc, yo, pull through all 3 sc on hook*. Repeat from * to * to end of round. Join, ch 1 (14 sc).
Row 28: 14 sc, join, ch 1. If you are going to stuff the body, do so now.

Row 29: *Draw up a loop in 2 sc, yo, pull through all 3 sc on hook*. Repeat from * to * to end of round. Join, ch 1 (7 sc).

Row 30: 7 sc, join, ch 1.

Head, Basic:

Row 31: To make the Basic Head, 7 sc, join, ch 1.

Row 32: 2 sc in each sc of round, join, ch 1 (14 sc).

Rows 33 - 35: 14 sc, join, ch 1.

Row 36: *Draw up a loop in 2 sc, yo, pull through all 3 sc on hook*. Repeat from * to * to end of round. Join, ch 1 (7 sc). If you are going to stuff the head, do so now.

Row 37: *Draw up a loop in 2 sc, yo, pull through all 3 sc on hook*. Repeat from * to * three times, skip last sc, join, ch 1 (3 sc).

Head, Profile:

Row 31: To make the Profile Head, 7 sc, do not join. Work Profile Head on page 47.

Arms: Make two. Work the same as the legs to R 10.

Row 11: *Draw up a loop in 2 sc, yo, pull through all 3 sc on hook*. Repeat from * to * to end of round. Join, ch 1 (7 sc).

Row 12: *Draw up a loop in 2 sc, yo, pull through all 3 sc on hook*. Repeat from * to * three times, skip last sc, join, ch 1 (3 sc). Cut yarn, leaving a tail that is 6″ long for stitching. Thread end into a darning needle and sew arm to body.

Breasts: Make two. Ch 3, join, ch 1.

Row 1: 5 sc in ring, join, ch 1.

Row 2: 2 sc in each sc, do not join, ch 1 (10 sc).

Row 3: *Draw up a loop in 2 sc, yo, pull through all 3 sc on hook*, 1 sc in next 4 sc, repeat from * to *, ch 1, turn (6 sc).

Row 4: *Draw up a loop in 2 sc, yo, pull through all 3 sc on hook*, 1 sc in next 2 sc, repeat from * to *, ch 1, turn (4 sc).

Row 5: *Draw up a loop in 2 sc, yo, pull through all 3 sc on hook*, 1 sc in last 2 sc, ch 1, and turn (3 sc).

Row 6: *Draw up a loop in 3 sc, yo, pull through all 4 sc on hook*, ch 1. Cut yarn, leaving a tail that is 6″ long for stitching. Thread end into a darning needle and sew breast to body.

Beaded hair for Profile Doll: Anchor a 20″ length of yarn to back of head by stitching in place a few times. Thread 11 wooden beads onto the strand. Take the strand of beads around the head. Stitch in place by stitching between each of the beads.

Paper beads: Bring the needle out at the side of the head, just under the wooden beads. *Thread a long paper bead and then go through a short one, and back up inside the long one, and into the head.

Bring needle out at position of next bead. * Repeat from * to * 8 more times. Anchor by stitching in place several times, then taking yarn inside head.

Looped halo of hair: Anchor end of yarn by stitching in place a few times at lower side of head.

Insert hook into a stitch at the side of the Head. YO, pull through and ch 10. Sc in next stitch on head. Repeat from * to *.

Finishing

1. Sew heart button to chest.

2. For Rose Zaftig Doll: Crochet and embroider face (see chart on page 23; instructions for embroidering on page 12) and stitch to head. Stitch buckle or large button to head.

The Hourglass Dolls

The Triangle shape is the source of a lot of inspiration. When you stack one triangle on top of the other, point-to-point, you get an hourglass. Here are some variations on the Hourglass Doll.

For the White and Rose-colored Hourglass Dolls, you will use the same pattern as the Button-joint Dolls for the head/shoulders and the Elegant Hands. See page 97. The Rose and White Hourglass dolls wear Random Lace Shawls; see page 40 for instructions on how to make them. Finished height of hourglass dolls: 11½" tall.
Gauge: 4 sc and 4 rows = 1".

Rose-colored Hourglass Doll ▶

Instructions

Beginning at the hem of the skirt, ch 42. Join, ch 1.
Row 1: 1 sc in each ch, join, ch 1 (42 sc).
Row 2: 42 sc, join, ch 1.
Row 3: [Draw up a loop in 2 sc, yo, pull through all three loops on hook]; 1 sc in next 17 sc; [draw up a loop in the next 2 sc, yo, pull through all three loops on hook] twice; 1 sc in next 17 sc, [draw up a loop in the next 2 sc, yo, pull through all three loops on hook], join, ch 1 (38 sc).
Rows 4 - 5: 38 sc, join, ch 1.
Row 6: [Draw up a loop in 2 sc, yo, pull through all three loops on hook]; 1 sc in next 15 sc; [draw up a loop in the next 2 sc, yo, pull through all three loops on hook] twice; 1 sc in next 15 sc, [draw up a loop in the next 2 sc, yo, pull through all three loops on hook], join, ch 1 (34 sc).
Rows 7 - 8: 34 sc, join, ch 1.
Row 9: [Draw up a loop in 2 sc, yo, pull through all three loops on hook]; 1 sc in next 13 sc; [draw up a loop in the next 2 sc, yo, pull through all three

Materials

- 4mm (G) hook
- Yarn, CGOA Presents: Frolic #08 Blithe #03 Kid Mohair #17
- Sewing machine thread: 1 strand each of: pale blue, rust, peach
- Wood veneer or paper for head and hands (see page 29)
- Pencil crayons for shading face
- Fabric glue
- Darning needle
- Cardboard for hat: 1 piece, 3" x 4" (mat board for picture framing is perfect)
- Scissors
- A half circle of stiff paper (the cover of an old calendar works great); the diameter of the circle needs to be 12", so you will need a compass that can open to a radius of 6"
- Craft stick

loops on hook] twice; 1 sc in next 13 sc, [draw up a loop in the next 2 sc, yo, pull through all three loops on hook], join, ch 1 (30 sc).

Rows 10 - 11: 30 sc, join, ch 1.

Row 12: [Draw up a loop in 2 sc, yo, pull through all three loops on hook]; 1 sc in next 11 sc; [draw up a loop in the next 2 sc, yo, pull through all three loops on hook] twice; 1 sc in next 11 sc, [draw up a loop in the next 2 sc, yo, pull through all three loops on hook], join, ch 1 (26 sc).

Rows 13 - 14: 26 sc, join, ch 1.

Row 15: [Draw up a loop in 2 sc, yo, pull through all three loops on hook]; 1 sc in next 9 sc; [draw up a loop in the next 2 sc, yo, pull through all three loops on hook] twice; 1 sc in next 9 sc, [draw up a loop in the next 2 sc, yo, pull through all three loops on hook], join, ch 1 (22 sc).

Rows 16 - 17: 22 sc, join, ch 1.

Row 18: [Draw up a loop in 2 sc, yo, pull through all three loops on hook]; 1 sc in next 7 sc; [draw up a loop in the next 2 sc, yo, pull through all three loops on hook] twice; 1 sc in next 7 sc, [draw up a loop in the next 2 sc, yo, pull through all three loops on hook], join, ch 1 (18 sc).

Rows 19 - 20: 18 sc, join, ch 1.

Row 21: [Draw up a loop in 2 sc, yo, pull through all three loops on hook]; 1 sc in next 5 sc; [draw up a loop in the next 2 sc, yo, pull through all three loops on hook] twice; 1 sc in next 5 sc, [draw up a loop in the next 2 sc, yo, pull through all three loops on hook], join, ch 1 (14sc).

Rows 22 - 23: 14 sc, join, ch 1.

Row 24: [Draw up a loop in 2 sc, yo, pull through all three loops on hook]; 1 sc in next 3sc; [draw up a loop in the next 2 sc, yo, pull through all three loops on hook] twice; 1 sc in next 3 sc, [draw up a loop in the next 2 sc, yo, pull through all three loops on hook], join, ch 1 (10 sc).

Rows 25 - 27: 10 sc, join, ch 1.

Row 28: 2 sc in first sc, 1 sc in next 3 sc, 2 sc in next 2 sc, 1 sc in next 3 sc, 2 sc in last sc, join, ch 1 (14 sc).

Rows 29 - 30: 14 sc, join, ch 1.

Row 31: 2 sc in first sc, 1 sc in next 5 sc, 2 sc in next 2 sc, 1 sc in next 5 sc, 2 sc in last sc, join, ch 1 (18 sc).

Rows 32 - 33: 18 sc, join, ch 1. Cut yarn, pull end through last loop on hook. Glue shoulders into body

Arms: Make two for the Rose dolls. Ch 4. Join to form ring.

Row 1: 4 sc in ring, join, ch 1.

Rows 2 - 12: 2 sc in first sc, 1 in each remaining sc, join, ch 1. At end of Row 12, cut yarn, pull end through last loop on hook and take end into sleeve.

Make wooden or paper hands and glue into sleeve.

Glue point of sleeve to shoulder.

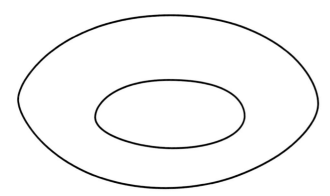

Covering the brim of the hat with yarn:

(Note that cabone rings are covered in exactly the same way.)

Cut brim from cardboard.

Holding hook on outside of brim: Reach into the center and pull a loop of yarn up to outside edge.

Reach back to the hold from the other side and pull up a loop pull through loop on hook.

Continue to draw up loops, and pulling them through the loop on the hook, alternating loops at front and back, all around brim.

Glue brim to doll's head.

Crown: Ch 3, join, ch 3, 11 dc in ring, join. Glue to back of hat.

Crochet a flower and glue to front of hat. See page 38 for pattern.

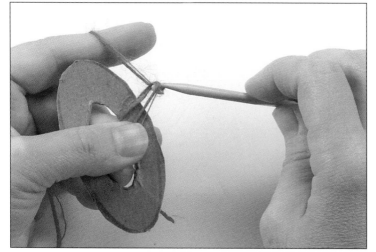

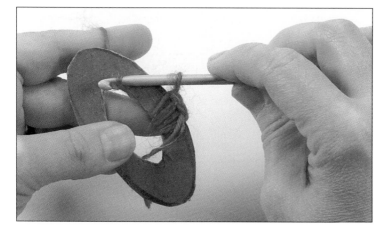

Materials

- 4mm (G) hook
- Yarn, CGOA Presents:
  Tropic #14
  Ritz White
  Kid Mohair #12, 13, 01
- Wood veneer or paper for head and hands (see page 29)
- Pencil crayons for shading face
- Fabric glue
- Darning needle
- Scissors
- A half circle of stiff paper
- A compass that can open to a radius of 6"
- Craft stick
- Stiff paper semi-circle to make cone to stabilize skirt
- Stuffing, small amount

▲ White Hourglass Doll

Instructions

1. Make two arms following Basic Arm instructions, but begin with ch 5. Make hands from wood veneer or paper and insert and glue into wrist.

2. For hair: Hold together 1 strand of each: CGOA Presents Tropic #14, CGOA Presents Ritz White, CGOA Presents Kid Mohair # 01. Make tufted wig (see page 35 for instructions), and glue to back of head.

3. Stuff torso of doll lightly.

4. Cut a semi-circle of stiff paper (I used the cover of an old calendar) with a radius of 6". The straight edge is 12" long.

5. Roll it into a cone shape.
Insert it into the skirt.

6. Glue skirt to paper cone.

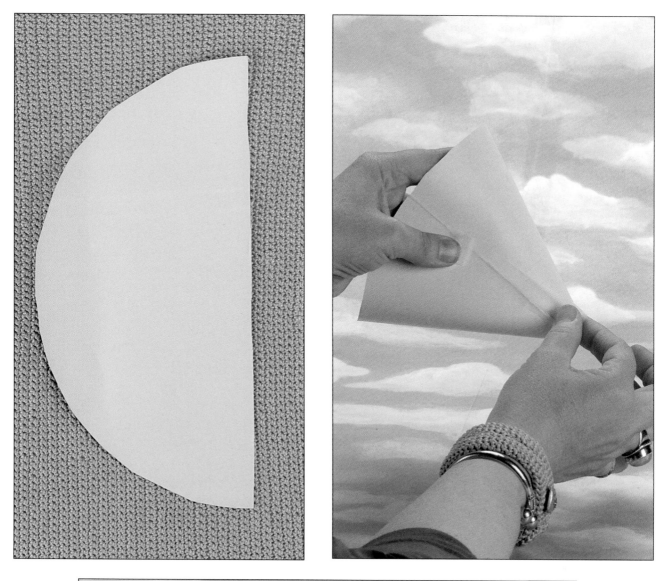

◀ Tapestry Crochet Hourglass Doll

Finished height of doll: 13". Gauge: 7 sc and 7 rows = 2".

Instructions

1. Make head and shoulders: Copy head and shoulders, front and back. Color with pencil crayons. Glue the head front to cardboard. When dry, cut out. Cut out head back and glue to back of head.
2. Make hands following instructions on page 28.
3. With rainbow yarn, ch 42, join, ch 1. Cut yarn, join black and white, and follow chart.
4. Sleeves: With background color, ch 4, join, ch 1. Follow chart.
5. Glue body and tops of sleeves to shoulder section of doll.
6. Crochet two small flowers with the background color of the dress, and glue to the backs of the shoulders.

Materials

- 5mm (H) hook
- Lily Sugar 'n Cream:
  Black #02
  Potpourri #178
  White #01
  Rainbow Bright #200
  Plum #07
  Jewels Ombre #201
- Paper for head and hands
- Lightweight cardboard for head and hands
- Fabric glue
- Scissors
- Semi-circle of sturdy paper to make cone for skirt
- Small amount of stuffing

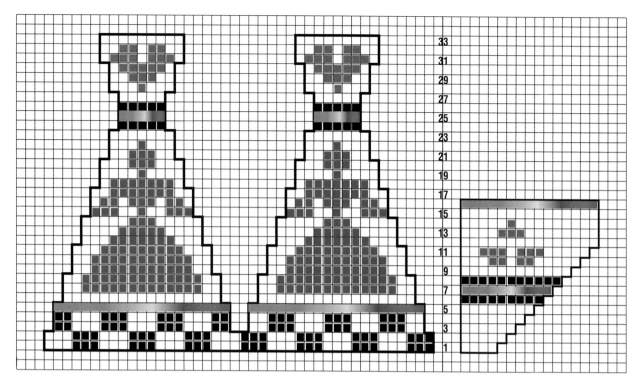

33
31
29
27
25
23
21
19
17
15
13
11
9
7
5
3
1

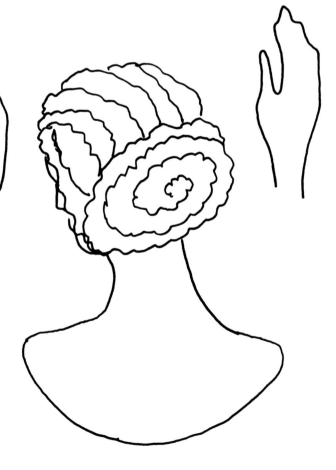

Materials for the Small Doll

- 1.5mm hook
- 5 strands of sewing machine thread held together

Materials for the Larger Doll

- 2.5mm hook
- Yarn, CGOA Presents: Frolic #11, #04, #09, #17
  Kid Mohair #17 and #18 for hair (l strand of each held together)
- For glasses: brass charms from Fancifuls Inc with blue paper glued to the lenses and touched up a little with a permanent black pen
- A little stuffing
- Darning needle

Triangle Bell Shape Skirt Doll ▲

When you play with the Hourglass skirt by taking out some of the repeat rows, you will have a shorter skirt with a sharper angle. The finished height of the small doll is 3½"; gauge: 12 sc and 12 rows = 1". The finished height of the tall doll is approximately 6", not including hair.
Gauge: 7 sc and 7 rows = 1".

Instructions

Begin with Leg # 1: Starting at the toes, with Blue yarn, ch 3, join, ch 1.
Row 1: 7 sc in ring, join, ch 1.
Rows 2 - 3: 7 sc, join, ch 1. Cut Blue, join White and Yellow.
Rows 4 - 15: 7 sc, join, ch 1. Work [1 R White then 1 R Yellow] 6 times. At end of Row 15, cut yarn, pull end through last loop on hook.
Skirt: Join Burgundy: Work R 1 - 4 in Burgundy.
Row 1: 1 sc in first 3 sc of one leg, ch 20, 1 sc in remaining 4 sc of the leg, 1 sc in first 3 sc of other leg, ch 20, 1 sc in remaining 4 sc this leg. Join, ch 1 (54 sc).
Row 2: 54 sc, join, ch 1.
Row 3: 11 sc, *Draw up a loop in 2 sc, yo, pull through all 3 loops on hook* twice; 1 sc in next 23 sc; repeat from * to * twice; 1 sc in next 12 sc, join, ch 1 (50 sc).

Row 4: 10 sc, *Draw up a loop in 2 sc, yo, pull through all 3 loops on hook* twice; 1 sc in next 21 sc; repeat from * to * twice; 1 sc in next 11 sc, join, ch 1 (46 sc). Cut Burgundy, join Teal.
Work Rows 5- 7 in Teal.
Row 5: 9 sc, *Draw up a loop in 2 sc, yo, pull through all three loops on hook* twice; 1 sc in next 19 sc; repeat from * to * twice; 1 sc in next 10 sc, join, ch 1 (42 sc).
Row 6: 8 sc, *Draw up a loop in 2 sc, yo, pull through all three loops on hook* twice; 1 sc in next 17 sc; repeat from * to * twice; 1 sc in next 9 sc, join, ch 1 (38 sc).
Row 7: 7 sc, *Draw up a loop in 2 sc, yo, pull through all three loops on hook* twice; 1 sc in next 15 sc; repeat from * to * twice; 1 sc in next 8 sc, join, ch 1 (34 sc). Cut Teal and join Purple; work R 8 - 10 in Purple.
Row 8: 6 sc, *Draw up a loop in 2 sc, yo, pull through all three loops on hook* twice; 1 sc in next 13 sc; repeat from * to * twice; 1 sc in next 7 sc, join, ch 1 (30 sc).
Row 9: 5 sc, *Draw up a loop in 2 sc, yo, pull through all three loops on hook* twice; 1 sc in next 11 sc; repeat from * to * twice; 1 sc in next 6 sc, join, ch 1 (26 sc).
Row 10: 4 sc, *Draw up a loop in 2 sc, yo, pull through all three loops on hook* twice; 1 sc in next 9 sc; repeat from * to * twice; 1 sc in next 5 sc, join, ch 1 (22 sc). Cut Purple, join Red: Work R 11 - 13 in Red.
Row 11: 3 sc, *Draw up a loop in 2 sc, yo, pull through all 3 loops on hook* twice; 1 sc in next 7 sc; repeat from * to * twice; 1 sc in next 4 sc, join, ch 1 (18 sc).
Row 12: 2 sc, *Draw up a loop in 2 sc, yo, pull through all 3 loops on hook* twice; 1 sc in next 5 sc; repeat from * to * twice; 1 sc in next 3 sc, join, ch 1 (14 sc).
Row 13: 14 sc, join, ch 1. Cut Red, join Yellow, and work R 14 - 18 in Yellow.
Rows 14 - 17: 14 sc, join, ch 1. If you wish to stuff her, slip a little stuffing inside her now.
Row 18: *Draw up a loop in 2 sc, yo, pull through all three loops on hook* 7 times, join, ch 1 (7 sc in round). Cut Yellow and join White (or any other skin tone that appeals).
Rows 19 - 21: 7 sc, join, ch 1.
Row 22: 2 sc in each sc, join, ch 1 (14 sc).
Rows 23 - 25: 14 sc, join, ch 1. Stuff head now.
Row 26: *Draw up a loop in 2 sc, yo, pull through all three loops on hook* seven times, join, ch 1 (7sc).
Row 27: *Draw up a loop in 2 sc, yo, pull through all three loops on hook* three times, skip last sc, join, ch 1. (3 sc) Cut yarn, pull end through last loop on hook.
Arms: Make two. Begin with White (or your skin tone of choice) and ch 3, join, ch 1.
Row 1: 6 sc in row, join, ch 1.
Rows 2 - 3: 6 sc, join, ch 1. Cut White and join Burgundy next two rows.
Rows 4 - 5: 6 sc in Burgundy, join, ch 1. Cut Burgundy, join Teal next two rows.
Rows 6 - 7: 6 sc in Teal, join, ch 1. Cut Teal, join Red next two rows.
Rows 8 - 9: 6 sc in Red, join, ch 1. Cut Red, join Yellow next two rows.
Rows 10 - 11: 6 sc in Yellow, join, ch 1.
Row 12: *Draw up a loop in 2 sc, yo, pull through all three loops on hook* three times, join, ch 1. Cut yarn, pull yarn end through last loop on hook.

Finishing

1. *Hair:* Note: Little Doll has loops of thread worked directly into her head as in the instructions for the looped wig on page 37. The Larger Doll's wig is made with two strands of kid mohair, following the instructions on page 37.
2. Sew arms to doll at shoulder.
3. Stitch or glue glasses charm to face, or make glasses with a wire or paper clip (see page 18 for instructions).
4. Embroider daisies (see instructions page 12) to her dress.

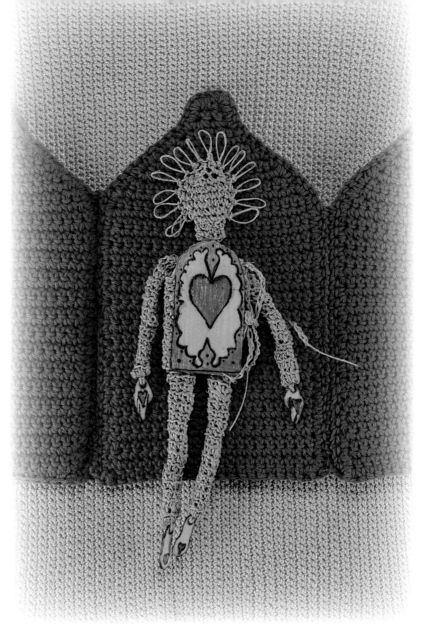

Pattern

Materials

- 3mm crochet hook
- Book: Card stock business cards glued to thin cardboard
- Fabric glue
- Sharp craft knife
- 1 ball thin hemp cord
- Mohair locks
- Darning needle
- 2 pieces of paper 8½" x 11"
- Scissors
- Paper clips or paper clamps to clamp covers while gluing
- Pencil crayons
- Black permanent fine tip marker or wood-burning tool
- 1 piece decorative paper for inside covers 4" x 41"
- 3 craft sticks
- Pencil

Book Doll

This is a book about dolls, so why not have a doll that is a book?

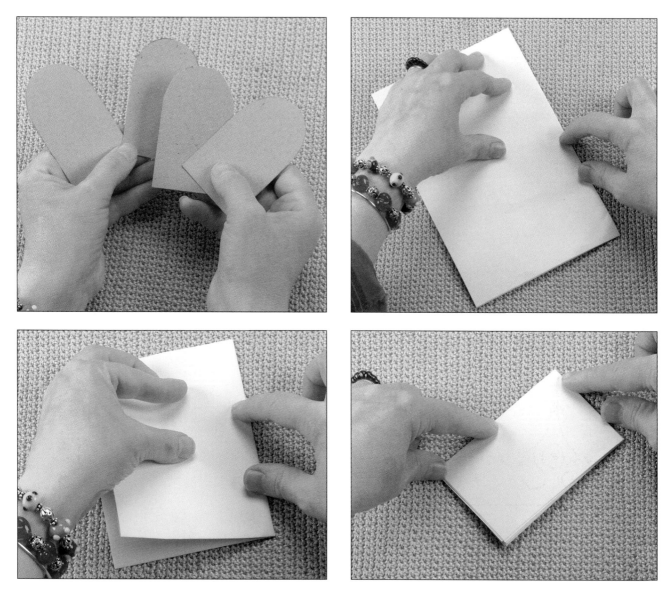

Instructions

1. Trace pattern onto cardstock four times and cut out.

2. To make pages: Hold the two pieces of paper together and fold them in half.
Then fold them in half again.
Fold in half one more time.

Trace around one of the pieces of cardstock with the pencil, and cut out.
Open the pages up and pierce the centerfold three times.

3. To make outer covers: Glue a business card, watercolor paper, or wood veneer to two of the cardboard pieces.
Clamp with paper clips or clamps to keep the paper or veneer from curling up.
Cut out the book shape when glue is completely dry.

4. Crochet the Spine:
Row 1: With the thin hemp cord, or your choice of yarn and a 3mm hook, ch 11, 1 sc in 2nd ch from hook (10 sc).
Rows 2 - 4: 10 sc, ch 1, turn. Cut cord, pull end through last loop on hook. Weave ends in.

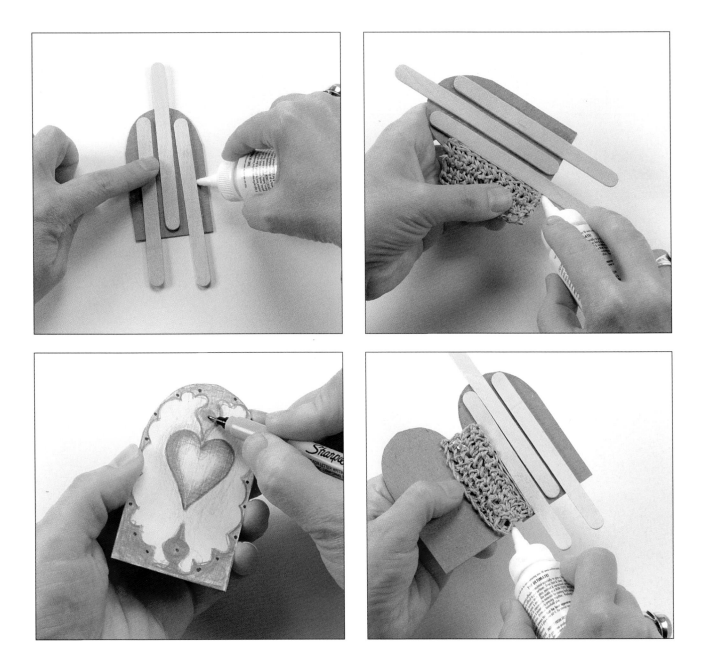

5. Glue the three craft sticks to the back cover.
6. Glue the spine to the back cover, right up against one of the sticks.
7. Draw and color the pattern onto the front cover.
8. Glue the other edge of the spine to the inside of the front cover.

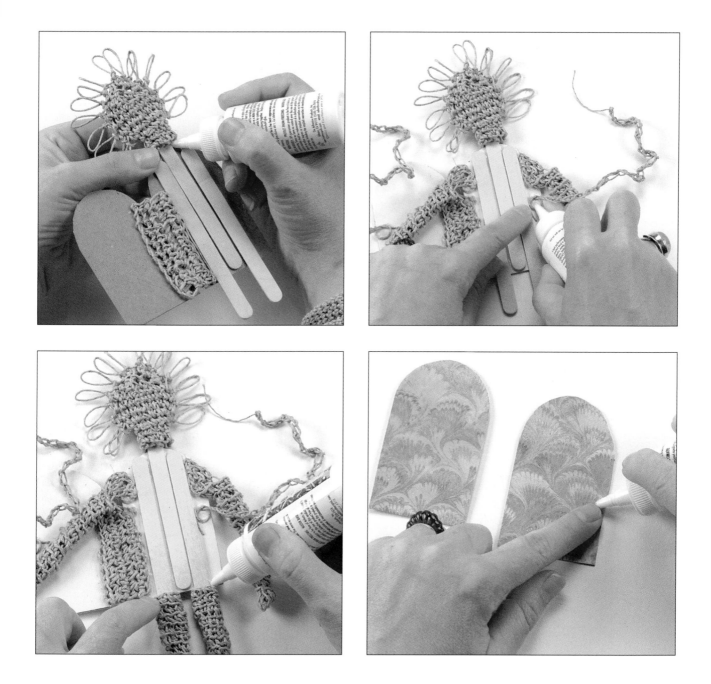

9. Crochet a Basic head, beginning at neck round. The Basic head has a halo of loops around the edge of the head, following the instructions for the wig with yarn loops on page 37. Glue head to stick.

10. Crochet arms: Work 11 rounds of 6 sc in the same manner as the legs. At end of Row 11, ch 3, turn and work 1 dc in next 2 sc to form shoulder tabs. Glue shoulder tabs to back cover.

11. Make two ties: Ch 30. Cut cord, pull end through last loop on hook. Glue to front and back covers.

12. Crochet legs: Work 15 rounds of 7 sc. Do not join the last sc of the round to the first, but work in spirals, working only in back bar of sc in previous round. Slip legs onto lower sticks and glue in place.

13. Inner covers: Glue decorative paper to the other two pieces of cardboard. Glue the inner covers to the inside of the outer covers.
Clamp with paper clips or clamps to hold in place until glue dries.

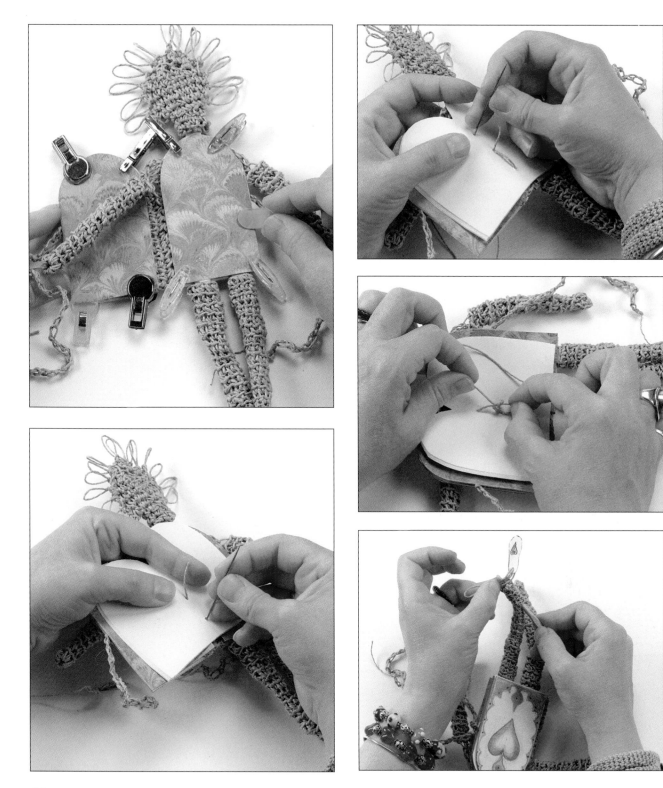

14. Stitch the pages into the crocheted spine: Go down through center hole and come up through lower hole.
Go back down through the center hole and come up through the upper hole
Tie a knot with starting end and trim.
(Note: When you fill the pages up, you can easily replace them by stitching new ones in.)

15. Make hands and feet #3 and attach to ends of arms and legs. See pattern page 32. Cut two 2″ lengths of cord per hand and foot, and take through the hole, then push inside end of arm or leg and glue in place.

Wild and Wonderful— Freeform Crochet Dolls

Freeform is a way of creating a crocheted piece without following a pattern. There are no set rules in freeform crochet, as each person defines her own way of working in freeform. One way of freeforming is to make many small elements (often called "scrumbles"), and stitch or crochet them together to build the finished piece. Another way is to make a foundation piece, and then attach the small bits to the foundation. This is the way that I have made this freeform doll.

I often base my designs on images that come to me in dreams, but this doll was really different. I had been working on her for a couple of days, and when she suddenly came together, there was a tremendous feeling of exhilaration. This happened just before I went to bed. Well! The Freeform Doll triggered amazing and wonderful dreams, full of incredibly inspiring imagery. I hope she'll do the same for you!

The doll in the photo was crocheted with two strands of Lily Sugar 'n Cream and a 7mm hook. This gave a gauge of 5 sc and 5 rows = 2". She was worked flat to make it easier to see where to place the small elements. The motifs, face, hands, and feet were all worked with one strand of Lily Sugar 'n Cream with a range of sizes of hooks. (3.5mm, 4mm, 4.5mm and 5mm hooks.) The feet are Noreen's Butterfly, folded in half and stitched to the end of the leg (see page 39 for instructions). The face is stitched using graph #1 on page 23. See the Instructions for hands, page 28; flowers, page 38; and coils for hair, page 104.

◀ Another Freeform Doll

I was so inspired by the first Freeform Doll that I just had to make another! This time, I decided to make her like the Long Skirt Doll on page 114. So, I worked a total of 24 rows with 14 sc before I began the shoulders, neck, and head. I used four strands of CGOA Presents Blithe #02 and a 4mm hook. I used a little bit of everything for the motifs. Her face is a carved avocado pit. See page 24 for instructions. See the Instructions for hat, page 69; hands, page 28; flowers, page 38; and butterfly, page 39. Her feet are two small pompoms.

In Conclusion

I have had the most wonderful time, designing and making the dolls for this book. It has truly been a delightful voyage of discovery. I hope that you will be inspired to crochet dolls that are an expression of your creativity, and that they make your heart sing!

Wishing you all the best, in all ways, always, with love …

Noreen

Resources
Web Sites

Noreen's Web site:
http://www.crone-findlay.com

The Crochet Guild of America
I asked Gwen Blakely-Kinsler, the founder of the Crochet Guild of America, to explain the CGOA: "The Crochet Guild of America was established to set an acceptable standard of work, and strive toward excellence in all facets of crochet; ensure the preservation of historical crochet projects and promote future crochet design ideas; promote the art and skill of crochet through exhibitions, continuing education, demonstrations, and seminars." Visit its Web site: www.crochet.org

Suppliers and Sources

Crochet Hooks
Turn of the Century handmade wooden hooks:
81676 Millsboro Road
Mansfield, OH 44906-3374
Phone (419) 529-8876
E-mail: Bill@Turn-of-the-Century.com
www.turn-of-the-century.com

Skacel Collection
For yarnstore nearest you:
www.skacelknitting.com

Yarn
CGOA Presents
PO Box 522
Belfair, WA 98528-0522
Phone: (360) 277-0710
E-mail: info@cgoapresents.com
www.cgoapresents.com/index.htm

Bernat/Spinrite
Lily Sugar'n Cream
www.sugarncream.com/

Patons Yarns
www.patonsyarns.com

Cedar Hollow Looms
Roving
www.cedarhollow.net/index.html
R.R. #3
Puslinch, Ontario
Canada N0B 2J0
Phone: (905) 659-1751
Fax: (905) 659-0125
E-mail: dow@cedarhollow.net

Fleece Artist
1174 Mineville Rd
Mineville, Nova Scotia
Canada B2Z 1K8
Phone: (902) 462-0602
Fax: (902) 462-0800
www.fleeceartist.com
kathryn@fleeceartist.com

kds fibres and textiles
PO Box 414
Ottawa, Ontario
Canada K1C 1S8
(613) 830-8675
www.kdsfibres.tripod.com

Brass Charms
Fancifuls Inc.
1070 Leonard Road
Marathon, NY 13803
Phone: (607) 849-6870
Fax: (607) 849-6870
E-mail: mailto:fancifuls@clarityconnect.com
www.fancifulsinc.com

Other Fibers
Lee Valley Tools
Nylon Cord, Jute, Raffia, Wood Veneer
1090 Morrison Dr.
Ottawa, Ontario
Canada K2H 1C2
Phone: (613) 596-0350
Fax: (613) 596-3073
www.leevalley.com

Heritan Leather & Crafts
Fine Hemp Cord, Copper Foil, and pin backs
120 Brock Street
PO Box 13,000
Barrie, Ontario
Canada L4M 4W4
Phone: (705) 728-2481
Fax: (705) 721-1226
leather@heritan.com
www.heritan.com

Craft Knives, Wood-burning Tool
Tools and Copper Ornaments
www.leevalley.com

Walnut Hollow
Versatool Wood-burning Tool
1409 State Road 23
Dodgeville, WI 53533-2112
Phone: (608) 935-2341
Fax: (608) 935-3029
www.walnuthollow.com/

Staples/Business Depot
Paper clamps and clips, pencil crayons
www.business depot.com

Boye Cabone Rings
www.wrights.com/

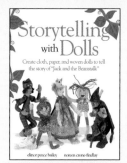

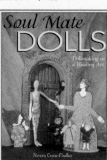